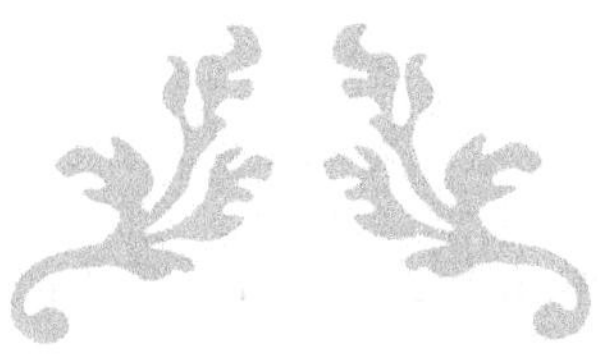

The Illusional Delusional Matrix Mind

a societal roadmap

2018
RECODED MINDS LLC
Colorado Springs, CO

The Illusional Delusional Matrix Mind

a societal roadmap

Mary Ann Schultz

ISBN:9781723072444
Recoded Minds LLC. Colorado Springs, Colorado

Table of Contents

Introduction

Throughout much of my life, I shared in the oppressive suffering that seems to plague our society. I was even diagnosed as clinically depressed. I spent years studying about the things that created my depression and learned that the "good life" that I was taught to believe in didn't match up with my personal reality. People didn't act the way that I thought they should, and I was very sad when people thought I wasn't good enough. As it turns out, the very lessons that society had led me to believe as "truths," not only were far from true, they were downright dangerous for my emotional, mental, and physical well-being.

To help illustrate my point in this societal exposé, it is my immense pleasure to include stories, quotes, and art from throughout time, which I call, "A Choir of Voices." I appreciate the rich tapestry that is created through these voices and artistry.

This book is a societal roadmap. It is my hope that the information will shed some new light on the boundaries of the experiences we call life. I hope that this information can help readers trade their conditioned delusional ideas for healthier happier ones.

This book is my gift to society; I hope that it helps create more kindness and compassion in this world. It is time for a paradigm shift, will you join me?

Thank you for reading,
Mary Ann Schultz, MA (Communications)

**Thank you to the following people and their representatives
for permission to share your work.**

Martin Luther King Jr.
Bruce Lipton
Stephen King
Malcolm Gladwell
Mark Nepo
Ram Dass
Wayne W. Dyer
Wm. Paul Young
David R. Hawkins
Buckminster Fuller
Sadhguru
Johann Hari
Edel O'Mahony
Sri Sri Ravi Shankar
Beth Hill
Mooji
Thomas Troeger
Barbara De Angelis
Jiddu Krishnamurti
David Evans
Warner Brothers
Styx – Dennis DeYoung
René Magritte
Nik Ainley (Cover).

PART I
WELCOME TO
THE GRAND ILLUSION

"So, if you think your life is complete confusion

Because your neighbor's got it made.

Just remember that, it's a grand illusion,

And deep inside we're all the same.

We're all the same."

Styx, the Grand Illusion

The Illusional Delusional Matrix Mind

"This world would be a whole lot better, if we just made an effort to be less horrible to one another." Ellen Page

I'm standing in a line of strangers; my obsessive thoughts wandering as I glance at the two well-dressed women in front of me. My hair is a mess and I am wearing an old pair of sweats which I had thrown on last minute to pick up the milk my husband forgot to buy. I start to feel very uncomfortable about my looks. *"They must think I'm a slob. I look disgusting."* At first, I berate myself until my ego can't take it any longer and the next thing I know, I am angry at my husband, *"I would not be standing here right now,"* I think to myself, *"if he had just gotten off his lazy butt and taken care of this like he said he would."* I even wonder if he loves me anymore. My thoughts are interrupted by the two women whispering and laughing together. Without a shred of evidence, I'm convinced that they are laughing at me. I feel extremely defensive and overcome with feelings of sadness and dejection, *"They're just a bunch of snobs with fake personalities,"* I angrily tell myself. As I leave, I feel nothing but the heaviness in my heart and the sadness rising inside me like a lake of sorrow until it overflows in a cascade of tears. The drama is complete.

The Illusional Delusional Matrix Mind has struck again. I have just been the victim of my own delusional thoughts. If we replayed the store security video, we would see a typical line of people and nothing more than an innocent interaction between two friends sharing a quiet laugh. The objective camera would not have picked up any interaction on my part at all and yet this had definitely become a part of my personal reality. My embarrassment, my anger, and my sadness toward my husband were all real. My thoughts and my suffering were part of my personal truth. In the end, my emotional and physical energy had taken a beating because my thoughts had created my reality. There could have even been a chain-reaction to this delusional event if I ended up passing on the brunt of my pain to the people I encountered next. The driving force behind this virtual-reality was nothing more than the thoughts in my mind, yet they were powerful enough to create realistic stories and, absolutely, real emotions. Our thoughts can and, often do, affect us adversely.

Perhaps it was my fault for having these thoughts in the first place. After all, it was clearly a case of "much ado about nothing." Shouldn't I have known better than to create a drama out of assumptions and conclusions? Well, to be fair, isn't this also the way of our society? Every one of those thoughts have been taught and modeled to me throughout my life. Many people can relate to this kind of thinking because it was part of our training, our upbringing, and our society. We relate to our thoughts getting carried away because we are familiar with this norm, but that doesn't mean we understand it. Although my thoughts were delusions, based on nothing more than illusions created in my mind, I had learned, along with most people, to believe what I think, and to allow delusional thinking to be a regular part of my life. Even though this way of thinking is considered normal, it brings a great deal of grief, confusion, and fear into our lives. The main reason we think this way in the first place is because horrible behavior is a societal norm.

This horrible behavior is an attribute of what I call, the Illusional Delusional Matrix Mind, a concept I have created using a paradigm model, in an effort to shed light on a very detrimental mind-set prevalent in society today. The model of the Matrix Mind paradigm was developed to help us understand some of the reasons behind why we are afraid and why we suffer. This way of thinking and behaving is hazardous to our peace of mind and our well-being. Most importantly, this way of thinking is completely optional.

As children, we first learn through the teachings and role-modeling of our parents, our teachers, and everyone and everything else in life that we observe and experience. Media and advertising fill our thoughts with their messages and agendas. These influences shape the ideas of who we strive to be, how we think, how we behave, and how we treat others. Unfortunately, many of the things that we first learn, and then act out in our own lives, are aspects of the Matrix paradigm.

Within the Matrix construct, we learn to focus primarily on ourselves, in the form of ego. We learn to believe what we think, and we acquire a list of expectations that we use to judge ourselves and others quite harshly. It is taught that our goal in life should be to make something of ourselves, to be successful - to be winners at all costs in order to avoid being "losers." To that end, we feel compelled to continually prove ourselves through accomplishments such as titles and wealth. For some, our defensive egos might seek to be better than someone else through a multitude of bullying practices including insults and gossip.

The court of public opinion is highly feared within the Matrix paradigm, yet we love to participate in it. We worry about what other people think about us, and at the same time, we are busy criticizing them. There is great fear in being wrong, so we often lie or deny when we make mistakes. We judge, and are judged, on an impossible bar of perfection. Subsequently, we become pretenders, posing and masquerading in an effort to convince the world that we are "good enough" while deep down inside we fear that we really are not. We believe that if we can convince others that we are actually special, they won't reject us. We crave acceptance and accolades from those around us. And yet, our defensive claws are always ready to attack the moment our egos feel threatened.

Happiness is elusive in the Matrix because we are often obsessed with past events and future goals. Even though there is nothing about the past that can be changed, we lose out on happiness by clinging to our suffering and forcing ourselves to relive unpleasant memories over and over again when things don't turn out the way we thought they should. Hate and victimhood are kept alive through the stories that we continually tell ourselves. It is not the past that actually hurts us; we suffer merely because we are conditioned to cling to and obsess over miserable memories. We further evade happiness by telling ourselves that we cannot be happy until we have met a next-to-impossible level of desires and goals that we were taught to expect in life. As long as we continue to rely on the custom that happiness is only found with the next lover, or the next job, or the next destination, or the next award - it will never be where we currently are. Our focus and joy becomes hijacked from the present moment as we regularly think instead about our past or our future.

Highly problematic within the Matrix paradigm is the concept that while dangling the goal of acceptance in front of us, we are actually being set up for failure. One of our main human objectives is to connect with one another, yet the Matrix not only divides us, it actually keeps us from thinking about each other. Since we each focus on our own ego, we seldom remember to be thoughtful or caring about anything or anyone else unless they personally affect us. We also spend a lot of time worried that we are far from good enough, so much so, that we miss out on true, meaningful relationships with others and we lose out on the main opportunities that life has to offer – the experience of our true, authentic selves.

Mike Jeffries, CEO of Abercrombie and Fitch once stated that he only wants attractive people wearing his brand.

"Nothing in the world can bother you as much as your own mind, I tell you. In fact, others seem to be bothering you, but it is not others, it is your own mind." Sri Sri Ravi Shankar

"Ego's idea of separation encourages you to base your worth on how frequently you emerge as a winner. As a hostage to your ego, self-respect is unavailable because you feel judged for your failures." Wayne W. Dyer

"Care about what other people think and you will always be their prisoner." Lao Tzu

"Curlers in your hair, shame on you." Television Commercial (1970's)

"It aint what you don't know that gets you into trouble. It's what you know for sure that just aint so." Mark Twain

What Are We Afraid Of?

"What is it that won't let us live our lives? What is inside of us that is so afraid that it keeps us from enjoying life?"
Michael A. Singer

We have all experienced fear. It is a human quality, automatic and hardwired into each of us. The fight or flight response is designed to protect us from physical danger. Fear is a reaction to the *thought* of pain and suffering. These days, since our basic needs are met, our fears are often based far more on our thoughts than on any actual dangers being faced in our lives. The fight or flight response will respond to any perception of danger, real or imagined. So the question is: what are we really afraid of? Interestingly, we are not only afraid of the things in life that might cause us physical harm, but we are also afraid of our relationships with others and even our relationship with our own selves.

Research indicates that some of the top fears faced in this society are: the unknown, pain, disappointment, misery, loneliness, confrontation, ridicule, rejection, public speaking, death, and failure. Notice how many of these fears deal with our thoughts about ourselves and what other people might think about us. We are afraid of being at the mercy of others, subjected to possible rudeness, meanness, bullying, and heart-break. We are afraid of these things because they are often prevailing elements in our current society and culture. Fear is a regular feature in our news organizations, and our society eats it up.

Much of this fear is created in our minds. Shakespeare wrote about "the slings and arrows of outrageous fortune." These slings and arrows are nothing more than a mind-set of illusionary weapons that we use against ourselves and others. Most of the suffering we experience in life is not from tangible wounds and is often not even based on current circumstances. It is through the focus in our minds that this delusional suffering is created. Many of the things that we fear, the things that create the greatest amount of suffering, are not real things at all. Indeed, many of those fears are merely thoughts that we are having in our own minds, illusionary vapors not found anywhere in nature. The thoughts inside our heads, concerning pain from the past or fear of the future, end up bothering us so much that they create suffering though there is no physical wound at all. These illusional delusions become metaphorical chains that bind us in a prison of our minds.

Why are we worried about the way that people will treat us and whether or not people will love and accept us? Why are so many of us afraid of one another? Well, it turns out that we have been taught and conditioned to believe and behave in a cultural mind-set of fear. This mind-set escalates as each bad experience plants new seeds of fear into our thoughts, creating a garden of paranoia, wherein we start to worry about everything that anyone does that might disparage us in any way. Within the Matrix Mind, we are more likely to fight each other or run away from each other than we are to accept and love one another.

Our fears often determine our actions. We try to control our circumstances through convincing people that we are good enough or by defending ourselves. Because of fear, we try to prove ourselves worthy of love and attention through stories of how great we are or by comparing ourselves to those we think we are better than. These comparisons can be hurtful to those around us, creating, and even spreading, more seeds of fear and paranoia. Furthermore, because we have tried to make others feel badly about themselves through our judgmental thoughts; we end up being afraid that people will do the same thing to us. We fear that they will exclude, belittle, mock or discount our very existence as they also attempt to make their own selves feel better. We become paranoid that other people's actions, looks and/or words are probably a direct assault against us…and so goes the vicious cycle of fear.

Ultimately, love and acceptance is what we all seek. We want to be happy and studies show that people are at their happiest when they feel accepted, connected, and an active part of humanity as a whole. In direct opposition to this goal, our Matrix prison feels more like solitary confinement. Many of us simply don't know how to connect with one another without the dark cloud of fear putting a damper on our emotions and thoughts.

The topic of fear is not new to humanity. It has been represented abundantly in our literature and music. Hamlet's soliloquy, which referenced the "slings and arrows of outrageous fortune," also speaks out about man's inhumanity to man and comes to the conclusion that life is "weary" to the point of the ultimate suicidal question of despair, "To be or not to be?" The rock band Rush created an entire symphony on the topic of fear. In the 1984 album *Grace under Pressure* there are three songs that are known as the Fear Series. These songs, "*The Enemy Within*", "*The Weapon*" and "*The Witch Hunt.*" refer to the unfortunate ways that we can miss out on life. The lyrics speak to the imaginary fears we create, the defensive behaviors we take on, the ways we attack and hurt each other, and the ways we spread hate, and consequently, fear through our judgmental thoughts and intolerance of those who are different. In writing these songs, Rush drummer and lyricist, Neil Peart adds his voice to a great many who are pointing out the power that fear wields as well as the devastation it leaves in its wake.

The movie, "The Spectacular Now," also highlights this sense of fear. Its main character, Sutter Keely, is a boy who is trying to escape fear by escaping personal connections in life. This leads him to the realization that escaping actually means missing out on life, as he describes in his college essay:

> "...the real challenge in my life, the real
> hardship, is me. It's always been me. As long
> as I can remember I've never not been afraid.
> Afraid of failure, of hunting people down,
> hurting people, getting hurt. I thought if I kept
> my guard up, and focused on other things, other
> people, if I couldn't even feel it, then no harm
> would come to me. I screwed up. Not only did I
> shut out the pain, I shut out everything, the
> good and the bad, until there was nothing."

We are living in a culture of fear, brought on largely by an overall confusion of what our lives are supposed to be about and confusion over how our relationships are supposed to be conducted. We are afraid of stepping on people's toes and of having our own toes stepped on. We are afraid of ourselves; afraid that we are just a bunch of posers pretending at life, and we are afraid that we will never be able to truly measure up. To make matters worse, we are afraid of others, afraid that they will not be able to truly measure up to the expectations that life has taught us to have of each other, and we are afraid of being left with nothing more than disappointment and heartache. Our fear has nurtured an environment of ill-will, dishonesty and mistrust which has led to further fear and confusion. We have become highly defensive amongst each other, which has led to a fear of true communication. This vicious cycle has created a society at risk, filled with anxiety, depression, and suicide.

A Choir of Voices
Fear

"The enemy is fear. We think it is hate, but it is fear."
Gandhi

Astronaut Buzz Aldrin's most-asked question: "Weren't you afraid?"

"The cave you fear to enter holds the treasure that you seek." Joseph Campbell

"Nothing in life is to be feared, it is only to be understood. Now is the time to understand more, so that we may fear less." Marie Curie

"To live a creative life, we must lose our fear of being wrong." Joseph Pearce

"Fears are educated into us, and can, if we wish, be educated out." Karl Augustus Menninger

Fear is only as deep as the mind allows. Japanese Proverb

"It takes strength and courage to live your truth in a world conditioned to fear." Edel O'Mahony

"You must be able to push on through the fear." Eleanor Roosevelt

Suffering of the Masses

"If you are distressed by anything external, the pain is not due to the thing itself, but to your estimate of it; and this you have the power to revoke at any moment."
Marcus Aurelius

We are currently living in a society so fearful that it seems emotionally and behaviorally unhealthy. Although our United States Constitution declares that we have the right to the pursuit of happiness, we are quite confused as to where true happiness can be found. Mired with problems stemming from fear, anger, and sadness, we are suffering from a culture in which hate, and depression permeate many aspects of our lives. Road-rage, brutality, bullying, self-harming, and suicide are examples of our plight. There seems to be a dark mood brewing throughout our society. As I was writing this book, there was a story in Panama City wherein residents were remarking on how the atmosphere of Spring break was no longer the mood of celebration and fun they had seen in the past. They said that they were witnessing a great deal of anger these days. That same afternoon, the top news headline was: 7 injured, 3 critically, in Panama City Beach Spring Break Shooting. Those residents could feel the problems brewing and remarked specifically on the change in the atmosphere. This cultural dark mood and discontent is being noticed and discussed by many of us. Actress Meryl Streep once gave her impression on current society by saying, "I think we are spinning out of control into chaos."

Let's take a look at some of our national statistics and see how "out of control" and chaotic things really are. The Centers for Disease Control and Prevention (CDC) provides our countries overall health statistics every ten years, most recently in 2013. According to this report, 24 million Americans suffer from depression each year. Suicide is the 10th leading cause of death in the United States and over 39,000 people die from suicide annually. In our schools, one in three students is bullied, while throughout our country 10 million people are physically abused, 85% of those are women. Approximately 15 percent of the population will suffer from clinical depression at some point during their lifetime. The financial impact of depression is also staggering. There are 17 million Americans a year consuming $11.3 billion in anti-depressants. Add to that the estimated $193 billion in lost wages annually, and the cost appears downright crippling.

Life is so confusing and overwhelming that we end up lashing out in anger at each other and ourselves. Anger and depression are major symptoms of an unhealthy mental state. Although some depression is caused by mental illness which is a separate part of the human story, it is quite likely that many of those who are angry and depressed are suffering primarily as a result of our crippling cultural mind-set.

My own personal story reflects these ideas. I spent many years suffering from what was eventually diagnosed as severe-depression. Over a period of years, different doctors asked me to try many different anti-depressants. They did not work for me because, as I told my doctors, the reason I was depressed was because my life was so depressing. I had suffered physical, emotional and financial abuse and was completely responsible for the support and upbringing of three young boys. Living seemed like an endless parade of impossible challenges. As society had taught me, I thought life was categorically unfair and that I deserved better. Being depressed made perfect sense to me as I focused on my pitiful circumstances through the eyes of the societal expectations I had learned to believe in. I was not suffering from a chemical imbalance; I was suffering from a societal imbalance.

These days, society is taking a closer look at bullying and suicide as stories relating the two are becoming increasingly mainstream. On January 12, 2012, 15 year old Amanda Cummings wrote a note about being bullied, tucked it into her pocket and jumped in front of a bus. She was not successful in her suicide attempt, but while she was recovering, her classmates added cruel posts on her Facebook page. Another example is Cynthia Sanchez who endured years of cyber-bullying including instructions on how to kill herself, which she did at just 14 years of age. In January 2018, two teenagers in Panama City, Florida were arrested and charged in the case of a young girl who hung herself. These stories have become more common as suicide rates among 10 - 14-year-olds have increased 50% over the last three decades according to the American Association of Suicidology.

The societal mind-set of fear, hate, and confusion is something we know well – we see it all around us, we hear stories of senseless beatings, murders, abuse and bullying. We are collectively becoming concerned as a society and are currently examining our laws and practices in these regards. Anti-bullying laws have been passed in 49 states. People all around are standing up to racial hatred and domestic abuse. As a society, we are beginning to recognize and take a stand against such atrocities.

Bullying seems to be a major premise in the story of our suffering. Many bullies are also in pain, as they too have often been bullied. The victims of bullies suffer physically, mentally, and emotionally. Victims feel powerless and fearful as they never know when the bully will strike again.

They are subjected to an array of attacks such as name calling, teasing, rumors, isolation, physical aggression, theft, and harassment. They can further suffer with trouble sleeping and frequent nightmares as well as addictions, weight problems and self-esteem issues. Bullying is not just a part of our school culture, it exists everywhere and it spreads suffering throughout our lives. Here is a distinction to understand bullying. If someone makes one disrespectful choice unintentionally it is referred to as rude. That same isolated incident done intentionally is referred to as mean. Disrespectful choices done repeatedly are referred to as bullying. Those who choose bullying tactics are often aggressive and do not like to be disagreed with. More and more, behaviors matching this description are rampantly spreading perpetual fear in our society.

Another extreme pressure causing anxiety and suffering comes from societal expectations. Ours is a culture that has high expectations for each of us as individuals. There is an expectation that we need to make something of ourselves, inferring that we are not already something and we won't be until we have hit some elusive mark. A lot of stress is created as well with the emphasis on being a winner and it's inference that if we don't win we are losers; and we really hate being losers! With these worries at hand, parents and schools, obsess about their children having every advantage at winning and being successful in life. This often results in children suffering from a set of stressful expectations. In a *Today* report about teenaged anxieties and self-harming, One teenager, self-described as "really stressed out" lamented, "From a really early age, I was exposed to the idea that if you don't get into a good college, you're gonna amount to nothing." Talk about pressure! The intense pressure that our society puts on us is dangerous. Another teen on the show shared how cutting "took her mind away from the emotional pain because something else hurt instead." To her, only physical pain could overcome the suffering that the stress and anxiety from high expectations was creating. According to the Cornell Research Program on Self-Injury and Recovery, nearly 1 in 5 college students have tried self-harming (cutting, burning, etc.). Our very own societal expectations and pressures are helping to create a society at risk.

Research has found connections between an unfulfilling life and addictions. Johann Hari, author of *"Chasing the Scream: The First and Last Days of the War on Drugs"* describes such a connection. Past studies, Hari explains, have focused on the addictive nature of substances, leading us to believe that the problem is in the substance. One such study showed test animals that were given a choice between drinking water and water laced with cocaine. The study showed these animals chose the cocaine water over the drinking water to the point of death, leading us to believe that cocaine is the reason for the devastating choice. A different study, however, challenges this assumption. This time they gave the same drinking choices to two sets of test animals. One set of animals was given a wonderful home and toys and friends, the other set of animals were given a solitary life in a cage. All of the animals had the choice of two water bottles, one with pure water and one with cocaine water. The animals that had a fulfilling life left the cocaine water alone for the most part and the animals in solitary confinement without any comforts became heavy users of the cocaine water. This research lends credence to the idea that our addiction problems might have a lot more to do with how extremely uncomfortable and isolated we are becoming in life. Hari speaks of our loneliness and states that, "we have created human societies where it is easier for people to become cut off from all human connections than ever before."

Most of us would agree that these trends are not indicative of a healthy society. We are failing at committed relationships and we are hurting each other with words and actions for no good reason. Even worse, we are killing ourselves and others. We are suffering inside and out on a massive scale. As with so much in life that is multi-faceted, there are many reasons behind depression and unhappiness including mental illness. This book is not meant as a comprehensive study of depression. It is, rather, a study of one specific contributor to our society's increasing unhappiness and dissatisfaction in life, the one which finds its roots and its fuel within the Matrix Mind.

A Choir of Voices
Suffering

"As a species we're fundamentally insane. Put more than two of us in a room, we pick sides and start dreaming up reasons to kill one another." Stephen King

"...expectations are the basis of guilt and shame and judgment, and they provide the essential framework that promotes performance as the basis for identity and value. You know well what it is like not to live up to someone's expectations." Wm. Paul Young

"Individuals mired in self -sabotaging beliefs." Bruce Lipton

"All of us have infinite potential but most of us are self-sabotaging." Mark Hansen

"We create our own unhappiness. The purpose of suffering is to help us understand we are the ones who cause it." Willie Nelson

"Someone's opinion of us can so easily trigger anger, sadness, even depression. Our sense of self is very ephemeral." Adyashanti

"People need to be right. If you can get that need out of your life, you'll save yourself lots of suffering." Wayne W. Dyer

There is No Box

"We are the architects of our own attitudes and experiences. We design the world by the way we choose to see it." *Barry Neil Kaufman*

Instead of limiting ourselves to the idea of thinking "outside of the box" we can open up a whole realm of possibilities with the understanding that there actually is no box. The "box' we refer to is nothing more than our societal norms, our paradigms. Once we start to understand the workings of the Matrix Paradigm as well as how detrimental it is to ourselves and others, we can't help but wonder about its place in society. Why do we buy into the suffering? The answer for most of us is that we don't know we have a choice. When our parents were born, they were taught their parents' beliefs and ideals, which likely included aspects of the Matrix Mind. These conditioned thoughts were reinforced in school and by society-at-large, and continued into their formative years and on to their parenting years without the knowledge that it was optional. This is how it was passed on to us. Generation after generation, Matrix ideals get passed on as though they are absolutes and there is no other way to live. We believe that our choices can only be found within the confines of society's mandates, also known as inside the box thinking.

Consider this story: A young, newly-married, couple was preparing a roast beef supper. The wife took the uncooked roast, cut off each end, which she threw away and then placed the roast in the pan. Thinking this was unusual; the husband asked her why she had cut off and thrown away the ends. Since it was the way her mother had always done it, she assumed it was the way a roast is supposed to be prepared. The wife then started thinking that it doesn't make sense to waste, so she called her mom and asked about the practice. Her mother had the same story and stated that she had learned it from her own mom and so with curiosity, she telephoned her mother to ask why. To that question the grandmother replied that she had only cut off the ends of the roast in order to make it fit her small-sized roasting-pan.

Often, we don't think about why we do things, we simply operate in the manner in which we have been taught. Society teaches us to conform. Many of us are conditioned to believe a very rigid set of ideals which, at times, include an unhealthy amount of Matrix expectations. Usually, we have no idea that there are choices and instead we go about life feeling imprisoned and chained by a mind-set that sets us up for failure and robs us of the excitement of living an authentic life.

What we don't understand is that the demands and expectations that we were taught are merely a matter of perspective. Although we are taught the concept of conformity without choice, we don't realize that there are a myriad of different ideas, concepts and norms found in the diversity of our society. Pastor and author, Rick Warren, puts it this way "Our culture has accepted two huge lies. The first is that if you disagree with someone's lifestyle, you must fear or hate them. The second is that to love someone means you agree with everything they believe or do. Both are nonsense. You don't have to compromise convictions to be compassionate." We seem to think that we always know the truth, when in actuality; all we can only ever know is our own personal perspective. Second century Roman emperor, Marcus Aurelius wrote, "Everything we hear is an opinion not a fact. Everything we see is a perspective not the truth." It is important to realize that we can only understand life through our own unique and limited perspectives.

Creative and imaginative thinking is often referred to as thinking outside of the box. The box, then, represents the constructs of society's way of thinking. Since these thoughts represent only perspective and not reality, we are left with the concept that there is no box at all. In actuality, we each have the freedom to choose the mind-set that makes the most sense to us. As nineteenth century, German philosopher, and cultural critic, Friedrich Nietzsche wrote, "You have your way. I have my way. As for the right way, the correct way, and the only way, it does not exist."

A Choir of Voices
There is No Box

"Rule your mind or it will rule you." Buddha

"Trade your expectation for appreciation and the world changes instantly." Tony Robbins

"Broken humans center their lives around things that seem good to them but will neither fill them nor free them. They are addicted to power, or the illusion of security that power offers." Wm. Paul Young

"Who knows what any of us sees from the privacy of our own blindness, and make no mistake, each of us is blind in a particular way, just as each of us is sighted uniquely." Mark Nepo

"You assist an evil system most effectively by obeying its orders and decrees. An evil system never deserves such allegiance. Allegiance to it means partaking of the evil. A good person will resist an evil system with his or her whole soul." Mahatma Gandhi

"During times of universal deceit, telling the truth becomes a revolutionary act." George Orwell

"The great masses of the people…will more easily fall victims to a big lie than to a small one." Adolf Hitler

PART II
Society ~ We the People

"Appearance is not essence,

perception is not reality,

and the cover is not the book.

Error is quite often convincing,

which is an unpleasant fact to consider and

accept. Everyone secretly believes

that his own personal view of the world is

real, factual, and true."

David R. Hawkins

Knowledge

"Wisdom begins in wonder." Socrates

"The only true wisdom is in knowing you know nothing."
Socrates

Our history is filled with questions about life. What is the purpose of life? Who are we? Why are we born? What are we meant to do with our lives? Who are we supposed to be? How are we supposed to act? What are we expected to say? Why don't other people do what they are supposed to do? Why do people say the ridiculous things that they say? Where is common-sense? Why are things happening this way? How much knowledge am I responsible for? What is true knowledge? Why can't we agree? Why is life so confusing? Why can't I get it right? What do any of us really know?

Let's face it; there is a whole lot to know. All knowledge is so vast and so deep and so wide that no single individual could ever come close to knowing everything. In actuality, the percentage of what the average human knows in comparison to all there is to know is statistically a tiny percentage ~ next to nothing.

The legacy of humanity is our total information. Collectively, we have gained and amassed an incredible amount of knowledge. For example, the British Library, in the United Kingdom, houses 170 million unique items, there are approximately 6,500 different languages currently being spoken on this planet and Wikipedia estimates that it would take over 96 million articles to cover the sum of everything we currently know. No single person can possibly know everything there is to know; it is all of us together who hold the keys to human knowledge.

Collectively, we, the people, are experts regarding all man-made systems presently in use, we have a working knowledge of every word in every language currently being spoken, and we are experts in every field of academic study throughout the world. Human knowledge is our legacy; yet individually we will only ever know a very small amount of that knowledge. Automobile mechanics know the workings of combustible engines while medical practitioners know the workings of the human body. There are individuals who are considered experts in all fields: physics, mathematics, health, geology, engineering, history, literature, philosophy, biology, sociology, business, political science, education, architecture, music, design and so on. The list is long, expansive and ultimately illustrates the point that the grand-total of human knowledge must be shared by many to be known at all.

We, as a human family, have been sharing, changing, utilizing and passing on the entirety of everything we know to future members since our beginnings. The reason we examine, grow and change our thinking is because much of our collective knowledge comes from our traditions, cultural norms, hypothesis and best-guesses. These are often based on the current focuses, trends and standards of society. As we examine things closely, we gain new insights and ideas. We sometimes discover that some of our ways of thinking, although they'd once seemed so certain, were actually flawed.

An example of a flawed belief system comes from a time when we believed that the sun and everything else in space rotated around the Earth. For hundreds of years, scholars poured their collective thinking and focus into this belief system. The idea that our home ground, the Earth, was the center of everything was very good for humanity. It translated into the thinking that human kind was also the center of the Universe, thereby "proving" God's favor. This mind-set was quite firmly planted in the existing way of thinking, especially in the minds of those in power. The people felt certain that their beliefs were absolute truths and anything else was not only a lie, it was sacrilege. Nicolaus Copernicus, a well-respected, 16th century mathematician and astronomer, was so afraid of the likely consequences he would incur for publishing his theory proposing that the Earth rotated around the sun that he waited until he was on his death-bed to release his writing. Luckily, his "scandalous" theory went unnoticed for a few decades, just long enough for fellow mathematician and astronomer, Galileo Galilei, to have a chance to read it before the church prohibited it. Regardless of the certain consequences, Galileo fearlessly went on to publish his own theory, boldly stating that the Earth actually rotated around the sun. These ideas were considered blasphemy against the church and God and he was subjected to trial by The Inquisition in 1632. At this same time another author, mathematician and philosopher of high regard, René Descartes, decided not to publish his similar findings based on the treatment that Galileo was being subjected to. Both Copernicus' and Galileo's publications were on the Index for Prohibited Books and not released in their uncensored form until 1835, almost 300 years after Copernicus first theorized that the Earth actually orbits the sun. Eventually, the ideas of Copernicus and Galileo could no longer be denied based on observations and experiences of the majority. Humanity was then free to think differently, to examine and grow knowledge in new directions.

Knowledge is defined as an awareness or familiarity, a person's range of information, or the sum of what is known. So, knowledge can range from everything in the universe that is currently known by all of us collectively to simply any bit of information known by any single person.

Human knowledge is not necessarily based in absolute
reality. Some knowledge comes as a set of ideas that can be
flexible and fluid as our beliefs and ideas change and grow.
Once we accept new insights, our existing ideas are open
for exploration and possibly change. We are then able to
seek out and follow new paths on our quest for meaningful
ideas and personal truths.

Our thinking will always be based on foundational
knowledge, which is not our own personal knowledge but
the knowledge of our people - our families, our
communities, and our cultures. "Truth," as we see it, is held
collectively. Currently, our society is embracing a very
unhealthy set of "truths" when it comes to Matrix-minded
thinking. But who is society? We are. Together, we decide
on the truths that we adhere to. Knowledge is determined
and selected by people and it is important to remember that
we are the people; we decide what we will believe is true.

Unfortunately, this seems to be a big secret. Instead of the
option to relax into the idea that there will always be more
to know than one individual can grasp, many of us grow up
with a sense that we are responsible for more knowledge
than we could ever grasp. We feel beholden to knowing
and saying all of the right things and making all of the right
choices in life. We also feel overwhelmed with this
responsibility because we find ourselves falling far short of
that mark of perfection on a regular basis. We live in fear
that we know less than we are supposed to know and we
worry that we are not up to society's standards.
It is possible that this was the very mind-set that author
Hans Christian Anderson wrote about in the children's
story, *The Emperor's New Clothes*. In this story, an
emperor was approached by two con-men posing as tailors.
They told the emperor that they had the finest fabric in the
land, one that could only be seen by the smartest people.

The con-men proceeded to show the emperor a bolt of imaginary fabric which he pretended to see in order to not appear stupid. The ruse played out over days, with each new participant pretending to see the garments, for fear of not looking as smart as everyone else, until the culminating event; a parade. During the parade, the emperor proudly walked along displaying his new suit of so-called "extraordinary clothes" until a young boy loudly declared that the emperor was naked. Fear had driven almost an entire kingdom to illogical conclusions and choices. Just like in this story, many of us will agree with what we are told because we fear that our own thoughts will prove us to be fools. We have been duped by the impossible concept that we can be held responsible for knowing it all.

A Choir of Voices
Knowledge
part one

*"Either there is no such thing as truth at all, or that
mankind hath no sufficient means to attain a certain
knowledge of it. It is therefore worthwhile to search out the
bounds between opinion and knowledge."
John Locke, "An Essay Concerning Human
Understanding." 1690*

*"We are what we repeatedly do. Excellence, then, is not an
act but a habit." Aristotle*

*"Learn how to see. Realize that everything connects with
everything else." Leonardo da Vinci*

*"Tell me and I forget. Teach me and I remember. Involve
me and I learn." Benjamin Franklin*

*"The more I read, the more I acquire, the more certain I
am that I know nothing." Voltaire*

*"I cannot teach anybody anything, I can only make them
think." Socrates*

*"Everyone you will ever meet knows something you don't."
Bill Nye*

"Now a few other very eminent and scholarly men made the same request, urging that I should no longer through fear refuse to give out my work for the common benefit of students of Mathematics." Nicolaus Copernicus

"All truths are easy to understand once they are discovered; the point is to discover them." Galileo Galilei

"To know that we know what we know, and to know that we do not know what we do not know, that is true knowledge." Nicolaus Copernicus

"We cannot teach people anything; we can only help them discover it within themselves." Galileo Galilei

A Kaleidoscope of Perspectives and Paradigms

*"Paradigms power perceptions and
perceptions power emotions.
Most emotions are responses to perception – what you
think is true about a given situation. If your perception is
false, then your emotional response to it will be false too.
So check your perceptions, and beyond that, check the
truthfulness of your paradigms."*
Wm. Paul Young, The Shack

Everything is a matter of perspective. Perspectives, like fingerprints, are unique. We can never know anything in the exact same way as someone else. Yet somehow we don't truly get a sense of this in society. Instead we often focus on "I'm right and you're wrong" and how things "should and should not" be. We end up thinking that there must be a correct answer to most everything and it is somehow our personal responsibility to be knowledgeable and compliant of these things. Many people get so caught up in their personal beliefs as ultimate realities that they end up fighting over them.

There is a classic tale of an elephant and six blind men. An elephant happened to be in town one day, and since the blind men did not know what an elephant was, they decided to go into town and have a feel. Each man touched the elephant and each one came out with a different perspective. One man said it was like a pillar while touching the leg. Another man disagreed saying it was like a rope as he held the tail. A third man said, "No, it is like a tree branch" as he felt the elephant's trunk. A fourth man held the animal's ear and described it as a large fan. The fifth man described a huge wall as he ran his hands along the elephant's middle. The men started to argue, each man believing that the others were wrong and that only his own viewpoint could possibly be valid. Along came the town's teacher who, when told of the circumstances, explained to the men that they were all correct about the parts, but they needed to share information in order to understand what the whole elephant was like. Our perspective and knowledge is only a small part of everything there is to know and all of the different ways that we can look at a situation. This story teaches us to recognize that our perspective is only one, of many different ways to understand life.

As a child I was confused regarding my own perspective because it seemed to me that I was "right" when people agreed with me and I was "wrong" when they disagreed, even though my mind was telling me that I was equally correct on both occasions. I felt lost and unsure as to whether, or when, I would ever get my thoughts in alignment with everyone else's. I was sure that somehow I was the one who was wrong and different. I grew up believing it was my job to learn everything that I was "supposed" to know and then be able to intelligently display a knowledge that is exact and true. I thought that if I studied hard enough, and asked enough questions, that I would eventually be the proud holder of the expected amount of knowledge. The more I studied, however, the more I recognized how very much there is to know, and that all I could ever know or understand would always be limited to what is in my mind and what I am currently able to focus on. I realized that I was actually right some of the time and wrong some of the time and I observed that everyone else was too. I started to understand that human knowledge was held collectively, shared by billions, yet still incomplete and imperfect, riddled with misconceptions and mistakes. I recognized that my own personal knowledge was just a tiny fraction of the whole, merely a matter of perspective, and only one of the many possible views of truth. I finally learned that all I would ever really

know would be my own imperfect truth, nothing more
nothing less, and that is all of us are in the same boat.
The idea that there can be multiple points-of-view is not
new. Many philosophers and academics have discussed the
concept that there are many layers of knowledge, beliefs
and understandings, and that actual truth is often elusive. In
the dialogue, *Protagoras*, ancient philosopher, Plato, wrote
that "Man is the measure of all things." This was a
controversial comment at the time because it was
interpreted to mean that there was no absolute truth except
what humans decided was true. This was problematic since
the prevailing paradigm of the time placed an emphasis on
the search for absolute knowledge. German philosopher,
Frederick Nietzsche, introduced the word *perspectivism* to
describe the idea that perspective is a way for each
individual to conceptualize the world and accordingly,
there are many possible perspectives. Nietzsche believed
that although there are different ways to perceive the world
around us, not all perspectives were necessarily equal. The
importance of perspective has been long studied throughout
history. In 1619, René Descartes was confused by the
illusionary nature of perception. He needed to convince
himself that there was an actual reality to be found. In the
end, the only reality that he could be absolutely sure of was
the reality of his own thought-processes which lead to his
famous declaration, "I think, therefore I am." Descartes
realized that since his thoughts could be manipulated by
him, they weren't necessarily real but that he, the
manipulator of the thoughts, must be.

Spiritual teacher and author, Eckhart Tolle, found meaning
in life through a similar experience which he shares in his
book, *The Power of Now*. As the title suggests, Tolle
discovered that only the actions we take during the current
moment can affect reality. He believes that all of the
thought-driven scenarios featuring the past or the possible

future are merely, "imaginary mind-projections." Tolle's "imaginary mind-projections" are much like the "illusionary delusions" referred to in this book.

These and many other stories share and build on the idea that our own personal perspectives can lead us to our own personal truths. We can never truly know anything beyond our thoughts; they are the lens through which we see the world. When it comes down to our personal truths, we are only able to make sense and gain understanding based on our own perceptions and the limits of our paradigms.

We use paradigms to organize our foundational knowledge. Paradigms don't naturally occur in life; we just use the concept of a paradigm as a model to show how certain things, once organized and sorted in a meaningful fashion, can be considered and analyzed from a less chaotic point of view. A paradigm can be described as a typical example, a distinct concept, an archetype, or an organizational template. It is a set of assumptions through which we view the world. Paradigms can be used to conceptualize specific aspects of human life often including societal beliefs, values, practices, cultural themes, worldviews, personal mind-sets as well as widely-held standards, norms, protocols, and taboos. Everything we have ever learned in life, all of our collective knowledge, can be organized into our various paradigms. We can use the model of paradigms to simplify our thinking, as a means of viewing and sharing reality, and as a guide to making personal choices. They are also used as a structural framework in research, businesses, academics and many other shared forums. For the purposes of this book, a paradigm is a mental construct or mind-set, a framework containing the basic assumptions, ways of thinking and methods such as rituals and practices commonly accepted by members of the group. These paradigms are contingent on our perceptions. Dominant

paradigms are contingent on shared perceptions within our society. Our paradigms are nothing more than a set of thoughts which create the foundational knowledge for everything that we value, focus on, and act upon.
Every aspect of our lives, our personal sense of self, our families, our relationships, our workplaces, our communities, and so on, can all be seen in terms of paradigms. For instance, everything we know about family stories, values, and traditions are rooted in the family paradigm.

Dominant paradigms, such as the family paradigm, include the perceptions, ideals, norms and beliefs that a majority of the people share. For example, one of society's most esteemed dominant paradigms is that of sports. We love sports in this country and most people know and understand at least some of the various attributes within the sports paradigm. The ideal of sportsmanship, for example, is a key attribute that includes a general shared meaning of competition within a code of honor and respect. Although it is true that sportsmanship is not always practiced in sports, we often see it as a reoccurring and poignant message of importance in many of our sports stories. Our words, actions, and reactions come together to help us create shared meaning. Our actions are often chosen by following the group's example. We learn to clap for a good effort or to shake our opponent's hand by watching what other players or fans do, and then doing the same. By accepting and using the established norms, we are providing a sense of conformity which we think will help us gain acceptance to the group. We also see how rejecting the norms of the paradigm can get us rejected from the group. A technical foul from a player or an overly disrespectful behavior from a coach or fan can result in ejection from the game completely. As we organize these common patterns of humanity we can see how they trend together. Thoughts and behaviors that influence large groups of people become parts of our dominant paradigms. Remember, paradigms are merely a manner of organizing and putting structure to our ways of thinking about the human experience.

Life can be explained and conceptualized through a myriad of paradigms, each one with distinct ideals and characteristics. We just saw, for example, how shared qualities and ideals create a standard of sportsmanship which is a key ideal within the sports paradigm. A closer look within that paradigm would display a myriad of other things such as: all of the sports records, the fans, the teams, all of the rules of all of the games as well as the games' cultures. Everything that we know and love about those games, such as baseball's seventh inning stretch, rivalries between teams, gold medals, or championship football parties; these examples are all part of the sports paradigm. Collectively, this paradigm would hold the facts, ideals and standards for all sports. Larger paradigms can be broken down into smaller, more specific paradigms for each individual sport. Sports' paradigms can even be broken down further into specific concepts like players, gear, merchandise, or even the beer-drinking habits of sports' fans.

Introduction to our first paradigms begins at birth. We learn about the family that we are born into, their language, their customs, their preferences, their fears and their knowledge. Specific to our families, we learn to love, nurture, care, communicate, teach, and protect. We realize our place in the family and the general expectancies had for each family member. The sum of our knowledge and beliefs regarding family can be seen as our family paradigm. Since each family is unique, the specific ideals, norms and standards for what a family "should be" differ from one family to another. Through life's experiences and lessons, we gain a working knowledge of other, key paradigms in our environment such as language, religion, sports, school, entertainment, self, and peers. All of our personal knowledge can be organized in this paradigm model. We are even beginning to see a trend of paradigm usage and talk about paradigm shifts in our society. Organizing our thinking in terms of paradigms can certainly help to disentangle chaotic concepts.

Most of us don't usually stop to question the origin or validity of the ideals found within our paradigms; we merely take them for granted and believe them to be true. Sometimes we do recognize that some of the things about certain paradigms don't make sense or seem to be flawed. Confusion can happen when conflicting standards and ideals from other people's paradigms and even from within our own, start to contradict each other and become illogical to us.

As we go about our lives, a multitude of paradigms are at work within our minds. These consist of everything we have ever learned and experienced. We are able to shift our focus from one paradigm to another without missing a beat. We have learned well the particular standards and protocols of work, home, and play. Our perceptions are often formed through the lenses of multi-layered paradigms such as language, family, work, personal ethics, media standards, and education. Dominant paradigms can be thought of as society's operating systems. They help create shared meaning, understanding, and expectations and they form the background knowledge from which many of us operate. They are the most influential to our conditioned-thought processes and are crucially important because we create our thoughts and choices in life based on the sum of our paradigms. This understanding can be a useful tool for examining the ideals and attributes of our own personal perspectives and paradigms.

Even society's issues such as racism, feminism, rage, depression, etc. are dominant paradigms within today's culture. The graphic on the next page depicts this model of paradigms as connected hexagons, much like a honeycomb. Unlike this static 2-dimensional model however, our true paradigms can influence, connect and combine with each other in various meaningful fashions. Each different combination brings a specific focus, which we call perspective.

A Section of Life's Paradigms

A paradigm shift in women's body ideals happened between 1950 and 1980.

Again, paradigms exist only in our thoughts and are subject to change as our thinking changes. Paradigm shifts happen when an existing paradigm no longer fits the current mindset. Let's take a look inside the paradigm of women's beauty and at our shifting perspectives regarding what society considers beautiful. In the 1950's for example, our society regarded voluptuous curves as the standard for beauty. Many women were shamed into thinking that it was unattractive to be skinny, as seen in the advertisement above. Marilyn Monroe's curvaceous size 16 was the ideal female body type and advertisers sold products to help skinny women pad on extra weight. A paradigm shift in the

1960's, saw an era that ushered in thin-as-a stick models such as Twiggy, and the societal norm for women's bodies changed drastically. Instead of trying to pack on more pounds, many people became negatively focused on fat and cellulite, which had gone from appealing to unsightly. Liposuction and diet aids were hustled in response. Eating disorders such as Bulimia or Anorexia Nervosa, the eating disorder which claimed the life of singer Karen Carpenter, have become common issues in our society due to our extreme focus on self-image. The ideals of the 50's and the 80's do not define beauty at all; they are simply a reflection of whatever shared opinions and standards are in place at a given time. These societal trends are often visible within advertisements trying to sell products geared toward the current standard of beauty. As soon as the majority mind-set and focus changes, the paradigm will shift accordingly. Some paradigms are tweaked others are replaced completely; they simply evolve in whatever direction humanity steers them.

Paradigm shifts also happen when our ideals and values run contrary to another paradigm. Racial paradigms have shifted and changed considerably in this country. Slavery was a strongly-held paradigm for 246 years before our national consensus agreed that it was unacceptable to treat humans in this manner and action was taken to create change. Later, the paradigm of Jim Crow laws and racial segregation in the south became a national issue. Rampant, inhumane treatment over four decades ultimately resulted in another paradigm shift when enough voices agreed that those laws were also unacceptable. Both paradigm shifts occurred because enough people were able to change their minds; they were able to see the Matrix ideals of hate and control as contrary to the ideals in other paradigms that teach kindness and respect. Many people stopped agreeing with a paradigm that allowed others to be treated inhumanly and traded that thinking for a paradigm which better mirrored their core values of love toward humanity.

Usually our paradigms are just there in our subconscious minds, invisibly contributing to our perspectives without bringing attention to the fact that they are actually running the show. It is during times of paradigm discontent and paradigm shifts that they really stand out. At these times, we can also more clearly see how related paradigms are connected. For instance, the examples of the two paradigm shifts related to racial inequity help us to see more about the connecting paradigms of both privilege and of basic human love. We can see how the paradigm of privilege, which allows one group more privileges than the other, played into the mind-set that felt comfortable with treating others inhumanly. Change took place when enough people were convinced by the paradigm of basic human love to stand up and make a difference. My personal hero, Martin Luther King Jr., strongly modeled the ideals of human love as he followed the example of his mentor, Gandhi, and advocated change of the Jim Crow laws by means of peace and love. He also demonstrated through his words and actions how much at odds a paradigm including love was to a paradigm including hate in saying:

> *"Violence never brings permanent peace. It solves no social problem: it merely creates new and more complicated ones. Violence is impractical because it is a descending spiral ending in destruction for all. It is immoral because it seeks to humiliate the opponent rather than win his understanding: it seeks to annihilate rather than convert. Violence is immoral because it thrives on hatred rather than love. It destroys community and makes brotherhood impossible. It leaves society in monologue rather than dialogue. Violence ends up defeating itself. It creates bitterness in the survivors and brutality in the destroyers." Martin Luther King Jr.*

In his search for a paradigm shift from hate to love, Martin Luther King Jr. demonstrated his belief that we are all connected and we are all important. We also see that we can collectively change our minds to create a better world. It is helpful to become conscience and aware of how our current paradigms affect and influence us. We can begin to appreciate how our different paradigms cause us to live in different versions of reality, a concept referred to as relativism by a man known for his work with paradigms, Thomas Kuhn. We can also gain an understanding of the requirements necessary toward moving out of the paradigms that do not serve us well and into those that offer happier, more peaceful outlooks.

Within this book, the Matrix Mind has been organized as a paradigm that qualifies as a dominant societal paradigm, one that invades and infects many of our other paradigms. Consider the ideals of the sports paradigm with its emphasis on good sportsmanship and playing an honorable game. When those ideals are over-powered by the ideals of the Matrix, such as "win at all cost" or "destroy your enemy," the sporting world can become dangerous and unfair. Athlete Lance Armstrong for example, went to extremely selfish and detrimental lengths in an effort to be the best in his sport. Armstrong admitted to lying and cheating his way to several Tour de France victories, stealing the win from other honorable cyclists who might have won a fair competition. Another example came before the 1994 Olympics when ice skater, Nancy Kerrigan, was clubbed in the leg as a result of a plot by the husband and the bodyguard of her rival, Tonya Harding. They were willing to resort to violence in order to get rid of the competition. The choices these people made were very contrary to the ideals found in sportsmanship, but they are quite familiar choices within the Matrix paradigm. The Matrix ideals of promoting egoic pursuits with messages such as: "be a winner," or "no excuses," can drive people to inhumane acts against self and others. Regardless of its negative impact on humanity, the Matrix paradigm continues to thrive because people believe in it.

A Choir of Voices
Perspectives and Paradigms

"It is our needs that interpret the world; our drives… Every drive is a kind of lust to rule; each one has its perspective that it would like to compel all the other drives to accept as a norm." Friedrich Nietzsche

In simple terms, the character of our life is based upon how we perceive it." Bruce Lipton

If you believe you can or if you believe you can't…you're right." Henry Ford

"Everything we hear is an opinion not a fact. Everything we see is a perspective not the truth." Marcus Aurelius

"You look at everything through the eyes of who you are." Chris Cuomo

"A man is but the product of his thoughts. What he thinks, he becomes." Mahatma Gandhi

"Your beliefs become your thoughts, your thoughts become your words, your words become your actions, your actions become your habits, your habits become your values, your values become your destiny." Mahatma Gandhi

"If you are really interested in knowing life in its depth, you must see how to enhance your perception." Sadhguru

"Sometimes people don't want to hear the truth because they don't want their illusions destroyed." Friedrich Nietzsche

Learning & Understanding

"Life can only be understood backwards; but it must be lived forwards." Søren Kierkegaard

We are born quite helpless, only able to communicate through primal means such as crying or squealing. We are unable to share in the language of our parents for at least a year and we aren't ready to care for ourselves for many more. These years in which we are highly dependent on the people who take care of us are the very years in which we learn the attributes and standards found within the prevailing paradigms of our families and our society. According to research on children's brainwaves, the human brain, from birth to six years of age, is specifically tuned for learning and at a very fast pace. Like a sponge, a child's brain soaks up qualities and conditioning from the various paradigms that he or she is exposed to.

Not only do we gain a working knowledge of our paradigms long before we know how to process our own thoughts, we learn them as though they are absolute truths. Usually we don't think to question the things that we have always considered "truths," until they start to create confusion. As we reflect on all that we have learned and all that we are exposed to in life, we start to see that not all "truths" are equally valid and some simply don't ring true at all. It might be helpful to understand how our thinking comes about in the first place and why many of us end up with that crazy mind that bothers us incessantly.

What's in a Mind-set?

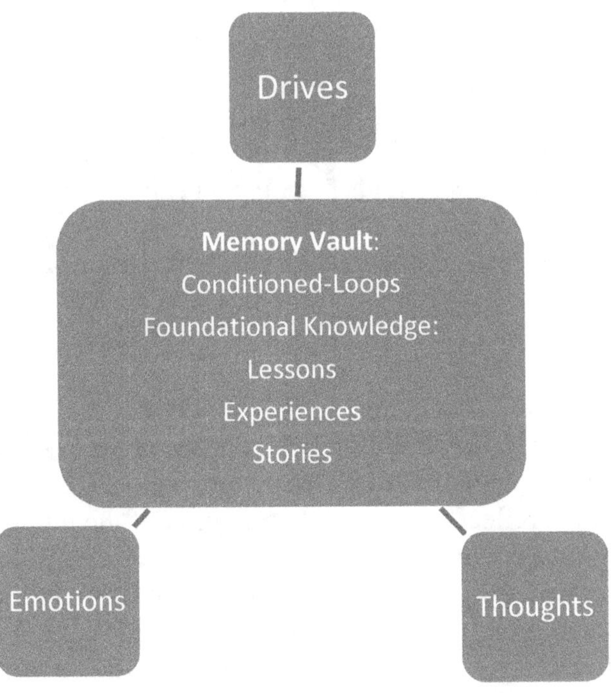

> **The conscious mind-set is composed of drives, emotions, and thoughts while the unconscious mind-set comes from the memory vault, which contains our conditioned loops, and our foundational knowledge.**

An overview of how we learn to imitate and formulate our thoughts can help us figure out how we think and why. Our drives, emotions, and thoughts are working together at various levels to create life choices and memories. Everything we choose to focus on as well as every action we take, every word we communicate, every emotion that we feel and every drive that we are willed to follow is created within the factory of the mind. Memories are not just about nostalgia; they are also the body's library of knowledge. Our memory vaults are filled with stories, conditioned-loops (a type of auto-pilot), skills, and lessons. Additionally, our minds have the amazing capacity to translate our thoughts into our own personal virtual reality. If you close your eyes and think about a triangle for example, you can make one appear in your mind's eye. The brain's capability of creating this "virtual reality" can help us come to terms with the fact that some of our thinking is, at times, not rooted in fact. We should not feel personally responsible, however, since our thinking is based on things we were taught before we were able to consider whether or not they reflect the truth. We can think of the mind, thoughts, emotions and drives, as a multi-use tool that can serve us best if we understand how to utilize it to our advantage. Without this understanding, our minds can become reckless, confused or even dangerous when they unravel down the road of irrationality.

Inside our brains we find thoughts and memories. Thoughts are messages created in our minds to ourselves. They are generated and processed according to the brain's encoding. Much like a computer needs programming in order to process a request, our thoughts are processed through our encoding, our foundational knowledge. Experiences provide information and data input to our minds. Enlightenment author, Adyashanti, writes in his book, *Falling into Grace*, "As we grow up, we learn this whole conceptual world, this whole way of thinking. We are brought up and initiated into the way that human beings think – the way they conceptualize life, the way they look at life – and bit by bit, as we grow up, we take on our culture's way of seeing life, of seeing ourselves, seeing each other, and also seeing the world at large." Notice how similar this is to the words of another enlightenment author, Don Miguel Ruiz, in his book, *The Four Agreements*, "We learned how to behave in society; what to believe and what not to believe; what is acceptable and what is not acceptable; what is good and what is bad; what is beautiful and what is ugly; what is right and what is wrong…all those rules and concepts about how to behave in the world." It is clear that we are influenced by our conditioning.

Our thoughts work on three levels; conscious, subconscious and unconscious. Conscious thought occurs when we actively focus our thinking. With focus, our conscious thoughts can create meaning, or perception, which is always based on some portion of personal knowledge and understanding. Through conscious thoughts we also create deliberate actions. The most active part of our brains, the subconscious mind, is responsible for our skills, knowledge and conditioned-loops. According to Dr. Bruce Lipton, author of *The Biology of Belief*, "the sum of our genetically programmed instincts and the beliefs we learned from our parents collectively form the fundamental programs in the subconscious mind." He goes on to stress the importance of subconscious programs since they are usually in charge of things. "The conscious mind runs the show, at best, only about 5% of the time." The subconscious mind, in charge 95% of the time, is based on our foundational knowledge, which is the basis for most of our mind's processing, our ideas, and our beliefs.

Fear and anxiety often create the mind that seems to always be in anguish. Called the monkey-mind by some, it is the talking inside our heads that sometimes won't shut up. Much of the incessant talking has to do with the fears we embrace. We have been programmed to reach for impossible goals for both ourselves and others. We have learned to focus on ourselves. We pay attention to the ways that life and people treat us, especially when they don't meet our expectations. Much of our suffering comes from our own minds, hyper-active with judgments and expectations, and regularly chatting away about everything that is wrong with the world. Another enlightenment author, Michael A. Singer, writes about the "chatter" inside of our brains in his book, *Untethered Soul*, as he asserts "when there is a buildup of nervous, fearful, or desire-based energies inside, the voice (in our heads) becomes extremely active. Talking releases energy. The narration makes you feel more comfortable with the world around you. Like backseat driving, it makes you feel as though things are more in your control." When our encoding is based in fear, and our foundational knowledge convinces us that we are not good enough, our experiences are not good enough, and our lives are not good enough, we end up feeling tormented and anguished.

Emotions can also run dangerously wild and rampant as a result of this kind of delusional thinking. In good times, emotions can be one of the best parts of being human, but when experienced through a mind weighed down with irrationality, our emotions can get hijacked into the illusional world. We are meant to experience the magnitude of emotions such as love, joy and peace, as a natural part of our humanity. We are born with the potential for every emotion and inside our minds we connect emotions with both drives and thoughts. When our thoughts are being driven from the Matrix paradigm, we often become irrationally driven by emotions of fear, anger and the like.

There is a connection between emotional reactions and the creation of memories. A strong emotional reaction to an event will often create a strong memory, attaching to it the energy of that emotion. Embarrassment, for example, is a strong emotional reaction and is often felt when we have made a public mistake, a time when people laugh at us or reject us which can make us think of ourselves as "losers." Chances are, every time you think about a specific memory that caused you great embarrassment, a flow of that same emotional energy surges right back along with your other thoughts regarding the event. You don't actually remember the event itself; you simply experience the virtual-reality copy that you encoded in your mind along with the emotional energy it contains.

Emotions can be quite an amazing and interesting part of our humanity. The energy that emotions bring to our experiences is like another one of our senses; we can literally feel the experience in our minds and bodies. Joy, awe, love, excitement, and surprise are just as important feelings as shock, fear, wonder and sadness. They all contribute to the full spectrum of our human experience. There are some emotions, however, that seem to add very little; rather, they can be quite detracting from the human experience. Emotions such as envy, hate, embarrassment, defensiveness, anger and jealousy are heavily promoted in the Matrix paradigm as normal emotional reactions to threats on our ego. These emotions have had starring roles in many high-dramas over the years, both real and imaginary, from reality television to Shakespearean tragedies and from trouble between friends to wars between countries. Emotions are part of our humanity; they are meant to be enjoyed, not to have control over us.

It is not mandatory that we go along with the cultural agreement that we should have strong emotional reactions to all of the things that society says we should. Once we understand how our thoughts and feelings are being formed and why, we start to realize that we have a choice in whether we truly wish to continue thinking and feeling along the lines that we've been taught. Indeed, once refocused, our thoughts and feelings can take on a brand new meaning and value in life. It is first a matter of knowledge and understanding and then simply a matter of choice.

The third component of our mind-set comes from our drives, will or volition. Our thoughts trigger reasons to activate our drives, telling us to jump into action. A couple of "growls" from our stomach for example, is usually followed by a thought about hunger which leads to some kind of an action like grabbing a bite to eat. Our drives are affected by various physiological events beside hunger. Our hormones are linked to aggression, depression, arousal and stress. Another very strong physiological response comes from the HPA axis (Hypothalamus-Pituitary-Adrenal axis) which reacts to a perceived threat by sending chemical signals through our bodies, resulting in the release of adrenaline. This is our bodies' fight or flight mechanism, which reacts to threats both real and imagined.

Rational thinking versus emotional thinking is often talked about and studied. It refers to thoughts that come from logical paradigms, whereas, emotional thinking often comes from our illogical paradigms, such as the Matrix. This is apparent in the concept of "comfort-food" which is something we are driven to eat when our emotional world needs a little comforting. This holds true for many of society's addictive behaviors; addictions have been linked to emotional discomfort. Our volition does whatever our emotional and at times irrational thought tells it to do. Actions occur as a result of focus and intent. Therefore, change can occur through focusing on our thoughts and looking at the encoding process to help us become familiarized with the nature and extent of the programs running our thoughts and beliefs.

I would like to share a personal story with a very instructive, "ah-ha" moment of clarity toward my own encoding. Long ago, I was suffering from a severe case of depression. I was using my own Matrix Mind as the basis for my thinking and suffering. Life was very confusing and I had become desperately sad about the way things were turning out for me. I met with a therapist who introduced me to the work of Aaron Beck, known as Cognitive Behavior Therapy (CBT). My therapist explained to me that inside my thoughts, I had put myself on trial in the courtroom of my mind. I had provided a top-notch prosecution, bent on ruining me; after all, that's the prosecution's job. What I had not done, according to my therapist, was provide myself with a defense attorney. He told me that I had every right, and indeed I owed it to myself, to present the other side of the story to the courtroom inside my head. I was focusing on all of the negatives and had neglected to think about anything positive such as the side of me that has many wonderful traits and brings goodness into the world. I had instead, painted a ghastly picture of myself. He was right! My line of thinking was not balanced, fair or even valid. That's when the light bulb went on. I started to understand that my way of processing thoughts was based on some very strange precepts and concepts that were not necessarily true or valid. Nonetheless, they resulted in some very depressing ways of thinking. I also realized that I had a choice on how I focus my thinking. If I focused my line of thinking on the inequities I saw in life, and based my thoughts on society's stories concerning not getting what I "deserved," I would feel sadness and despair. Comments such as, "You don't deserve to be treated that way" conditioned me to believe in a victim mentality. When I learned to focus my thinking instead on what was currently happening in the moment, I usually found happiness and joy. As it turns out, life is pretty good most of the time. What I have discovered, is that my peace of mind and happiness depend on which set of thoughts I choose to focus on.

The next piece of the puzzle fell into place when I realized that much of my thinking came, not from my focused, conscious thought, but from my subconscious thinking. Through reading and studying the ideas of many authors, I became acutely aware of the role that encoded, subconscious thoughts, beliefs and ideals played in the creation of my thoughts as well as in my overall focus. I began to realize how much my encoding dictated my ideas and expectations about myself and everything else. Many of the "rules" of society that I had been solidly taught and which I had solidly believed in now seemed random, judgmental, unkind and unnecessary. Unfortunately, I also found them to be solidly instilled in my thinking processes, stuck as solidly in my mind as every painful memory that had been processed through my Matrix thinking.

"Practice makes perfect" is not at all true, but there is truth in the twist, "Practice makes permanent." Repeated exposure eventually creates conditioned loops in our minds. These loops have basically the same emotion and the same message each time we think about them. Pet-peeves and sad memories are examples of conditioned loops. Habits of mind, such as repeated opinions, judgments or stories, are all conditioned loops as well. Many of our loops are created as a direct result of being regularly exposed to other people's paradigms. Conditioned-loops are created as part of our mastery in learning. Anything we know how to do without having to think about is a type of conditioned loop. As author and teacher Adyashanti wrote, "You don't even have to be consciously thinking about it because it is so deeply woven into the fabric of your perception." Remember the example of an embarrassing memory that can bring back the emotional feel and energy of embarrassment? Well, that is also an example of a conditioned-loop. We have been conditioned to process life through our egos and through a set of strongly-held beliefs and expectations regarding what we deserve and how we think people should or should not treat us. When those expectations are shattered by an oppositional event such as someone not treating us as we think they should, we often respond primarily in our thoughts. We tell ourselves stories highlighting all of the reasons that the other person is wrong and how they are guilty of mistreating our feelings. These stories often include our expectations of how we think that person should have treated us. We have learned to combine these thoughts with the emotional reaction that we feel is appropriate for the drama at hand. If we feel like a victim for instance, we might feel sad, mad, or fearful, much like I felt that day at the grocery store in chapter one. Conditioned-loops get stored in the subconscious mind with all of the energy, emotion and drama from which they were created. There is a super-charged memory that can bring back virtually the same drama and emotion every time we think about them. Someone's memory, for instance, of being humiliated and embarrassed by a spouse's infidelities, can bring up pain and suffering even years after the divorce! As long as our thoughts continue to feed the message that we did not deserve to be treated this way or that way or, worse yet, secretly fearing that maybe we did deserve to be treated badly, as long as we feed ourselves this mind-set, we will be haunted by our unpleasant memories and thoughts. The emotions that accompany this kind of thinking can dictate the quality of our lives. That is the nature of our worst conditioned loops. It is also the nature of the Matrix paradigm.

Conditioned-loops have various effects in our lives. A pet-peeve is a mild version of a conditioned-loop, for example. These are things that irritate us every time we are faced with them. Examples such as becoming upset over people not holding the door open for us or not bothering to say "thank you" when the door is opened for them, or becoming upset at things such as traffic lights or driving habits, basically anything that bothers us every time we encounter it is a conditioned-loop. Most pet-peeves are accompanied by negative energy. We can become upset, merely at the thought of something we disagree with. There are positive conditioned-loops as well, such as the sentiment of "God bless you" whenever someone sneezes. We don't really think about the words, we just say them as a reaction to the sneeze and as a way to show we care. Through repeated exposure, our foundational knowledge is created and becomes our bases for beliefs and behaviors. These beliefs lead to issues and problems that can become stronger and more poignant the more that we focus on them. Our thoughts feed our fears and make them stronger, eventually turning them into permanent sources of suffering.

We also learn our basis of thought and behavior through repeated exposure to our role models. This consists of everyone we are around, especially on a regular basis. Babies and young children are always watching, observing, and learning how to imitate. They closely watch their parents and other family members, their teachers and anything else that captures their attention. The tendency to get our cues from those around us does not end in childhood. There was a young man who was not on speaking terms with his brother because differing perspectives had led to misunderstanding, defensiveness and animosity. He was discussing this situation with his father who retorted, "I don't understand why you boys act this way, we taught you to be kind to each other." The young man thought about this and realized it was true that he was taught to treat others with kindness. He also realized that he and his brother were acting very much like he had seen his father and uncles act toward each other. The old saying, "Do as I say, not as I do" is a faulty parenting method as it seldom works. For positive change to take place, we owe it to each other to be the best role models we can be.

Our foundational knowledge is also created through the social conditioning of reward and consequence. Known as operant and classical conditioning, we become conditioned to think or behave in specific ways in certain circumstances in life. Operant conditioning occurs when a cause and effect relationship is established in our thoughts. The old adage, "once bitten twice shy," illustrates this concept as it is usually true that once we have been bitten by something painful we will learn a conditioned response of shying away from whatever bit us and from anything that our mind connects to the bite. As I stood on a Key West beach looking at the beautiful waters that I had been excited to snorkel in, I also saw a great many translucent blue sails bobbing in the water. With more than a few memories of very painful jellyfish stings coming to my mind, interest in swimming amongst the Portuguese men-of-war was reduced to dread. In other words, my painful jellyfish memories had conditioned me to fear and avoid the possible mistake of putting myself in a position to be stung again. This is the concept of operant conditioning. Everything that rewards us or punishes us has the potential for a corresponding conditioned-loop inside our minds. The more painful an experience or the more repetitions we experience, the stronger the conditioned-loops will be.

Our society teaches conformity through promises of rewards and punishments. If you are a good boy, you will get candy; If you are a bad boy, you will get a spanking. Societal rewards include things like gifts, monetary rewards, acceptance, conditional-love, hugs, praise and the like. Unfortunately, these rewards often come with strings attached. Take the idea of Santa Claus for instance. Children are taught that they better watch out and behave or they will not be on the list of "good children" and won't get their heart's desires. This is also an example of how our thoughts can be conditioned in regards to punishment. Acts such as the withholding of gifts, money, love or acceptance are forms of conditioning through fear. Behaviors such as the show of disapproval, disgust or even hate along with acts of aggression are all ways in which conditioning happens through fear. We end up in a society that seeks happiness through rewards and suffers from the fear of possible punishments.

Regrettably for most of us, the rules of society and how we are supposed to be as a person are encoded and imprinted upon us as absolute truths. Many of our leaders and teachers are convinced that their beliefs and ideals are absolutely true and they pass them along as such. This tendency can be thought of as "inside-the-box" thinking. We become engrained with the ideals and standards that society embraces and since they are taught to us as absolute truths, we have little reason to question. Eventually, the student becomes the teacher and armed with a head-full of "absolute truths," they pass that same foundational knowledge on to the next generation.

Since most of our concepts of reality and truth are based on foundational knowledge, it would help to start with healthy concepts in the first place. Parents are typically our first teachers. As they talk to us and to others, we learn their language. We learn far more through their attitudes and examples than we do through their direct instruction. Children watch and listen for years and then they imitate what they learned for a lifetime. The movie, 42, highlighted how easily children are taught prejudice for example, as a young boy begins his day excited at the prospect of seeing the famous Jackie Robinson but soon finds himself yelling racial slurs along with his daddy. The boy had no feelings or thoughts of hatred or animosity until he saw it modeled by his father. Children follow the examples of their parents, first and foremost, because it is the source of their primary security. Parents often believe that children should do as they are told and obedience to parents and conformity to their ideals and beliefs is usually a key attribute to the family paradigm. Insistence on obedience instills traits of conformity which ensure that a parent's ideals and beliefs will be instilled, or encoded, in their children.

Parents send their children to school with the expectation that they should learn and conform to the paradigms of our educational system as well. Children trust their parents and since their parents trust the educational system, so do the children. Teachers and principals also have an expectation of general conformity within the school model. In 1944, The Bridgeton Public Schools published a school annual stating that the overall goal for students was that they learn the necessary qualities for leadership, citizenship and "conformity to the decisions of the majority which rules." We have many reasons for conformity in school, which at times makes sense for safety and learning. Unfortunately however, it also teaches us how to blindly follow norms of thinking, acting, and behaving. Children are told what to do, when to do it, how to sit and these days how to take a test. We pass on the ideas of conformity without much thought as to why we do these things and whether or not they are in the best interest of the children or even humanity as a whole.

We learn a lot of social protocols, but the one with the most impact concerns the information that we are taught about self and the concept we describe as ego. From our earliest memories, we are taught to think about ourselves from the point-of-view of other people's acceptance. Comments such as, "what a pretty girl" or "what a strong boy" become important indicators of our feelings of worthiness. We are taught to seek out approval as a means of gaining information or social acceptance. Our society promotes the idea that it is our mission in life to succeed and make something of ourselves, to be somebody someday. We learn that the only way to do that is to be better than average, to be a winner. In the meantime, we learn to worry that we are not good enough. We learn that one way to gain acceptance is through displaying and advertising our best traits. The need to appear physically and mentally at the top of the game can lead to feelings of phoniness and inadequacy. We also learn to defend our egos from rejection through fight or flight reactions. Our egos learn to fight through defensive or offensive tactics such as outrage, criticism, condescension, bullying or gossip. Or, we learn to run away from these issues in unhealthy ways such as procrastination, complacency, apathy, cutting, or suicide. We go through all of this simply because we were taught that we are supposed to focus on ourselves and on being a winner in order to be worthy of love.

We learn many of the details of our various paradigms through our media. Famous, American, filmmaker, George Lucas, referred to those in the motion picture industry as "teachers with loud voices," and actor Alan Rickman referred to them as "agents of change." Movie lines, lyrics, celebrity quotes, and advertising jingles, all get encoded as part of our mind-set. We learn how to talk, how to dress and how to behave through these various examples.

We learn many Matrix messages through media and advertising as well. We are flooded with stories that often focus on drama and the craziness of Matrix attributes all the while reinforcing the negative messages in our minds. Advertisers use aspects of conditioning such as catchy slogans and songs to make their product permanent in our subconscious minds. They try to condition us into believing Matrix ideals such as the impossible bar of perfection. Current commercial mentality for instance, would have us believe that "sexy" is something we should all aspire to, but of course it can only be achieved through spending money. In an effort to look the part, we are taught to buy clothes, jewelry, make-up, and so on. At times, we even subject ourselves to dangerous pills and surgeries. The messages we receive are often detrimental to our physical, emotional, and mental well-being, but we are buying into them nonetheless, because they have become a part of our encoding, part of our very thoughts. Advertisers know that they can teach you to buy their products, and that is why they will spend around $220 billion in 2018 alone.

Throughout our lives, we learn to think in many ways, always based on our existing paradigms. As we have seen, some of our thinking comes from unhealthy concepts and paradigms. This can lead to poor decision making and can affect how we view the world. Cognitive biases are a large part of our thinking. A cognitive bias is a tendency toward an irrational idea or an idea based on illogical inference. As it turns out, our societal paradigms are filled with cognitive biases such as stereotyping, group-think, or egocentricity.

Like the old adage, "we are what we eat," we are also what we learn. The biases that we are surrounded by are likely to become the ideas that we believe as truths. Stereotyping and prejudicial thoughts are widespread in our current culture. When we grow up surrounded by messages about "them" such as: they are lazy, they are emotional, they are unintelligent, or they are dangerous, we grow up believing that these beliefs are actually truths. Stereotyping is just one such bias that plays a major role in creating illusions and delusion in our thinking.

There are many biases that affect our ability to find logical answers or truths. Confirmation, salience, placebo, overconfidence, blind-spots, and bandwagon are a few examples of the many cognitive biases we are subjected to. Group think, for example, is a term used for the bandwagon bias, wherein a group of people believe they can come to the "correct" answer merely by consensus. In 1986, group think was directly connected to the space shuttle Challenger disaster that cost seven lives. Although a leading scientist warned the launch committee of the dangerous possibilities connected to the O-rings, the committee believed that the political implications to cancelling the launch were so great that they could not risk being seen as alarmists and so they would risk the lives of the astronauts instead. This tragedy illustrates that going along with others for the sake of agreement and not being open to outside information can keep us from finding the truth. Sadly, many people find their truths through consensus and end up blindly following the norms, sometimes at great expense.

Society's thinking is strongly influenced by these cognitive biases. Win our extreme focus on ego, we have been taught to believe what we think. Critical thinking experts, Dr. Richard Paul and Dr. Linda Elder state that, "Egocentricity means confusing what we see and think with reality. When under the influence of egocentricity, we think that the way we see things is exactly the way things are. Egocentricity manifests itself as an inability or unwillingness to consider others' points of view, a refusal to accept ideas or facts which would prevent us from getting what we want." As people are socialized, egocentricity partly evolves into sociocentricity. Egocentric tendencies extend to their groups and affiliations. The individual goes from "I am right!" to "We are right!" Richard Paul and Linda Elder state that, "Uninformed thinkers often confuse loyalty with always supporting and agreeing, even when the other person or the group is wrong." So we end up believing what we think, without allowing new information to inform our thoughts, and end up agreeing with the ideas of those who are important to us, even when we know they are wrong.

Rules, laws, norms, tribal beliefs, tribal rituals, customs, agreements, stories/dramas, compliance, and conformity: these things are the foundation of our encoding. Our paradigms are constructed from everything we have learned in life. Together, they are like a playbook for life. Within this playbook, we find "rules" for how we should think, talk and behave. The rules are not real, they are more-or-less guidelines, and not every group shares the same guidelines, nonetheless, we end up using our "rules" as a measurement for judging, as a way to determine "right" from "wrong."

Believing what we think comes from the assumption that knowledge is static, real, and tangible. We believe that there is a right answer to everything and that most of what we think and believe reflects reality and truth. Many of us end up believing that it is our responsibility to have the right answers, which we rarely do, so we end up feeling like a failure. We become fearful that people might find out that we are far less than perfect, so at times, we put on a mask and pretend to be as good as everyone else, even though inside we believe ourselves to be worthless.

Sometimes, experience brings us to a point in life where we question our paradigms. We see attributes that make no sense and we start looking for answers. The good news is that we are never too old to learn; after all, at age 85, Renaissance artist, Michelangelo, proudly declared, "I am still learning." Many people even consider life's lessons to be the main point of living. Our conditioned loops and paradigms are subject to change at any point where we decide to change our minds and our ways of thinking. As Socrates stated, "The secret of change is to focus all of your energy, not on fighting the old, but on building the new."

A Choir of Voices
Learning and Understanding

"Man has a pretty static picture of the world, accidentally or forcibly imprinted upon him by means of chains of conditioned associations. Man believes his imprint board is reality." Timothy Leary

"Our lives are essentially a printout of our subconscious programs, behaviors that were fundamentally acquired from others before we were six years old. As psychologists recognize, a majority of these developmental programs are limiting and disempowering." Bruce Lipton

"There is a dimension to life that is not fully knowable simply by our rational capacities. I love reason, I love science, but reason doesn't explain to me what it feels like to kiss my wife." Thomas Troeger

"Till a man can judge whether they be truths or not, his understanding is but little improved, and thus men of much reading, though greatly learned, but may be little knowing." John Locke

"Your beliefs become your thoughts, your thoughts become your words, your words become your actions, your actions become your habits, your habits become your values, your values become your destiny." Mahatma Gandhi

The Paradigm of Language

"We should have a great fewer disputes in the world if words were taken for what they are, the signs of our ideas only, and not for things themselves." John Locke

The paradigm of language is meant as a tool for human communication and understanding. Every language has a set of attributes and protocols, such as alphabets, words, sentence structure, grammar, and punctuation, which are put together in an attempt to create shared meaning. Words are just as symbolic within our minds as perspectives and paradigms are; they are used to help us describe our thoughts but they are not reality themselves.

French painter and social activist, René Magritte, tried to share this concept in his painting "Treachery of Images." The words on the painting are translated, "this is not a pipe." Magritte is sending the message that we can easily mistake symbols for reality. After all, that is certainly not a pipe; it is merely a painting depicting an image. Without this understanding, many people might argue at length that it is, in actuality and truth, a pipe. The word "pipe" is as symbolic as the image in the painting, simply a word meant to portray an idea. Words are merely symbols for something else. It can be treacherous to human understanding and communication when we rely heavily on imperfect symbols and imperfect perspectives as a perfect match for perfect meaning.

Many of us become over-confident, believing that our language and thinking skills are so masterful that we can use them as a way to ascertain what is real and true in life. We can get so lost in our minds' attempt to second-guess and analyze other people's words and actions that we end up misunderstanding, and then fear keeps us from asking simple, clarifying questions. Oftentimes we rely only on our thinking processes to ferret out "true meaning" instead of engaging in meaningful fact-finding conversations. Language came about as a tool to create shared meaning. If we get lost, however, in our ideas and our perspectives regarding the symbols and how they are "supposed" to be used, especially when other people's usage and understanding differs from our own, we can easily forget to pay attention to our responsibilities of good communication. We might, for example, pay more attention to someone's misuse of a word than in the message that person is trying to convey. When language is used for something other than shared communication, we often end up with distorted, and at times, disastrous results. Through learning and conditioning, we end up with basic mastery over the language of our society. No one bothers to tell us that there is much more to language than we will ever know, so we are left with the illusion that we actually do know it all. Many of us honestly believe that we are completely capable of comprehending other people's messages based solely on our own thinking and understanding. Because we speak a common language, we get a false sense of confidence in our communication skills. We don't necessarily understand that language and meaning is encoded in each of us differently, thereby creating differing perspectives. Instead, we get stuck in the confusion created by our differences and we focus on who is right or wrong in place of simply trying to gain better understanding. We are rarely taught the importance of listening and speaking with a goal of clarity and shared-meaning.

From birth, perhaps even earlier, we first experience, then imitate and learn our home language. It becomes encoded in our minds as conditioned-loops. Our word choices, our syntax and even our accents are all conditioned in our subconscious minds as permanent memory. We usually don't have to think about how to speak or which words to use as we comfortably go about our conversations using speaking skills from a subconscious level. Except in times when we have reason to choose our words carefully, speech comes to us as second-nature. The ability to speak freely while on conversational "auto-pilot" is an example of our conditioning. We even have conditioned sayings such as "God bless you" or "bye" which we use regularly without much thought.

It's an interesting side-note that the term "bye," something we think of as simply a nice thing to say as we leave, is actually an example of an historical paradigm shift in language. Five hundred years ago, the "correct" terminology was "God be with ye." The adolescents and young adults of the time began employing the shortened version, "good-bye" much to the outrage of their parents. At that time, the idea that "God" was being omitted from the language was scandalous. What was once a highly controversial choice of words, is now commonplace and acceptable language. The important concept to know about language and meaning is that we, the people, make it whatever we want it to be.

Language would be easier if we used it only as a tool, but unfortunately, we also learn to use it as a weapon. In today's mind-set, the old sayings, "It can't hurt to ask," and "Sticks and stones may break my bones, but words will never hurt me." can seem untruthful to the multitudes who suffer great heartache over the words of others. Much of life's meaning is conveyed to us through the use of symbols. We learn to use words, such as labels and descriptions, as a means of stereotyping things. In our society, it is common to label people by their color or race as a means of identification. I was talking to a friend for example, about a new student that I had in my classroom, a refugee from the Ivory Coast. I was asked if the girl was African-American, to which I answered that, no, she is an African girl, not American at all. This led to the true question: "I meant, is she black?" I found it to be an interesting question and I wondered why that fact even mattered? Sure, we describe each other regularly using many descriptors such as black, white, big, fat, tall, skinny, short, and so on, but what is the purpose of knowing these details? Do we describe others as a matter or clear communication, or do we describe others as a means of judgement and possibly discrimination? Through words we often create a sense of value-laden judgments. I don't blame my friend for asking, she was simply thinking along the societal lines from which she was taught. Another way we are taught to label people is by using the words that describe their actions as a way to define them as people. If we make a choice that society deems to be a good, bad or stupid, we might be labeled from that choice as being a good, bad, or, stupid person. The words that we learn to use and the inherent value that we attach to those words become a major aspect in our foundational thinking. The societal trend of defining people by their looks or by their actions plays a powerful and often damaging role in our mentality of us versus them.

Much like our habit of believing in the absolute nature of our thoughts, we also have a tendency to believe in the absolute nature of our words. We learn in school that there are language rules to be followed and that there is an absolute right way of using language, otherwise it is clearly wrong. Our thinking is also influenced by the polar nature of the English language. As our brains are wired to notice things that are different from the norm, our language teaches us to put judgement and value on those differences. We are taught the thinking skills of compare and contrast. We look at how things are similar and how they are different and then we define them accordingly. We are taught that something can be explained or defined by both its synonyms and its antonyms, which conditions us to think in polar extremes. For instance, if we are in a competition and we are not the person to finish first, not only are we not the winner but we are also the opposite of a winner, we are a loser. This may seem like only a matter of semantics, but when we get lost in the symbolism and start defining our own self-worth through these words and comparisons, we tend to define our imperfections as failures and that often becomes the basis for suffering. Many of us are afraid to try something new for fear of not succeeding and being labeled as a "failure." The tendency to use language as a means for judgmentalism is one example of how words can become abusive and lead to suffering.

Although words are merely symbols, we use them to tell the stories that eventually become our personal versions of reality. Communication expert, Walter Fisher, wrote several essays on a communication theory that he termed "the Narrative Paradigm." He created his paradigm as a model for human understanding by means of determining truthfulness through our stories. Fisher describes the qualities of storytelling as a way to conceptualize both communication and life. Whether a story has fidelity or "rings true" is the cognitive process used to determine if a story makes sense according to a person's own beliefs. As we experience life amongst other humans, we notice that stories are often used as a way of sharing life with one another. Dramatic stories are modeled, pitied, and celebrated widely throughout our media outlets. We often talk to ourselves in story fashion as well. Our stories become a part of our thinking and our perspective. Memories are usually stored in the form of stories as well. We use our stories to compare, interpret, and understand our lives.

Our personal histories are organized through our stories. Many of us remember events such as the spaceship Challenger exploding, or the Twin Towers crashing down, through the stories of our own lives. For example, the morning of September 11, 2011, I had just dropped the kids off to school and was headed to work. While listening to the radio, I heard a real-time narration of the second jet flying into the second tower of the World Trade Center. I wondered if it was real, or simply like Orson Welles' *War of the Worlds*, the 1938 radio broadcast that caused a nationwide panic. That night we watched the towers implode on television, over and over. Even though we were told that it was real, I kept thinking about how much it was like a Hollywood movie. I remember the story this way every time someone brings up 9/11. We each create the stories that narrate our own lives.

When it comes to telling our stories, we can easily fall short on clarity. The ability to communicate in a very specific fashion is difficult for many of us. Instead, we often communicate in quite general terms and think that our listeners will understand our specific meaning. Differences in perceptions, along with unclear or unspecific communication, often lead to misunderstandings. Our chances of sending out a general message and having it understood in the same specific way that we are thinking, is very slim. This concept is illustrated in professor of English and U.S. Senator, S.I. Hayakawa's, "Ladder of Abstraction." If I merely asked you to think about a ball, you might be thinking about a baseball, a crystal ball, or even a Cinderella ball. The word ball without any context is quite general and could become confusing, which is why it is towards the bottom of the ladder of abstraction. As the ladder rises, the field of words becomes more narrow, specific and clear. A sample set on the Ladder of Abstraction for the ball in question might look like this: {sphere, ball, game ball, sports ball, tennis ball.} If I wanted to research tennis balls on the Internet, it wouldn't make any sense to search by "sphere" or "ball." We have learned to be very specific in our Internet searches yet we still struggle when it comes to clear and open communication in our human interactions. Problems can arise when we don't choose our words for clarity or if we don't ask questions regarding understanding. It's no wonder that there is so much difficulty with open honest communication. Because we learn to be fearful and mistrusting in our conversations, we find ourselves walking on egg shells or beating around the bush as necessary norms of "safe" conversation. The fear of putting people on the defensive keeps many of us from asking clarifying questions. Between our unclear dialogues and our unshared personal perspectives we end up with crazy-difficult communication issues. We are unaware of how often our words are perceived differently than we mean them, and we are afraid of the honest conversations needed to facilitate understanding.

Throughout much of written history, scholars have warned that words can be subject to perspective, misuse and manipulation. Ancient Greek philosopher, Aristotle, introduced the study of logic and warned us of the practice of language abuse over 2,300 years ago. He famously described various fallacies that are used as means of unfair persuasion and he laid the groundwork for discerning logical communication. One fallacy, which Aristotle called a false dichotomy, is "you are either with us or against us." We hear this and many other illogical statements passed as truths all the time. In 1690, English philosopher, John Locke, wrote about language misunderstandings and abuses. He described the confusion created by the ambiguity and imperfections in words and the "willful abuse of words in order to deceive." Those who try to manipulate things by lying and cheating are focusing on Matrix ideals and have no problem twisting the meanings of words and ideas to suit their egoic self-interests. For thousands of years, scholars have been describing and warning against the abuses of language, yet these problems continue to plague us as a people. Aristotle and Locke both tried to lay the groundwork for more honest and meaningful communication that could lead to an arena of mutual understanding; unfortunately it hasn't yet caught on. Instead of building on the lessons of a clear and logical foundation for communicating, we seem to live in a time of overwhelming confusion and misunderstanding.

Along with words, we are also taught about body language. When we converse, approximately 80% of meaning is derived from non-verbal communication. This includes aspects such as the way we sit or stand, the way we hold our arms, the direction of our gaze, and the tone of our

voice. Perhaps it is true that we have a tendency to cross
our arms when we are short on patience, but we also tend to
cross our arms when we are cold or when we are standing
and our arms want a place to rest. A major tenent of
research within the social sciences is that, when studying
people, we cannot present our findings in absolute terms
because when it comes to people's behavior, thoughts and
beliefs, there are no absolutes. Yet in popular media, we
see studies that put people into boxes all of the time, and
are translated as truths to be adhered to. A recent article in
Forbes online titled, "10 Worst Body Language Mistakes,"
is an example of how generalities in human nature become
twisted into expectations and contribute to the impossible
bar from which we have learned to judge ourselves and
others. If you were to use this article as a guide, you would
think that there is reason to mistrust or avoid people who
slouch, have either too-weak or too-strong of a handshake,
fold their arms, angle their body any direction other than
straight forward, fidget with (or even touch) their hair, or
stand too close. Good eye contact is a must and you are
perceived negatively if you are looking down, away, or
even at a clock. The article teaches that these actions
indicate discomfort, self-consciousness, anxiety, disinterest,
arrogance, deception or disrespect. Such value-laden
descriptions stated in absolute terms can leave readers with
the impression that there is truth in the idea that we can
define other people by their actions and, for ourselves that
we should worry about every action we make because
people might come to faulty conclusions about us as well.
Articles such as these teach its readers that these things are
completely true and a necessary focus in life. This is part of
the lie that society is suffering under. We do not have to
think along these lines. If we have a reason to keep track of
time, we should be able to look at a clock without someone
judging us as rude. And if we are cold, we should be able
to cross our arms without someone judging us as bored.

When we buy into a mind-set, we are beholden to it.
Making choices outside of an unhealthy and disrespectful
mind-set is not only optimal for peace of mind; it also leads
to more positive role-modeling. We have a choice between
a healthy and an unhealthy point-of-view. It's all a matter
of perspective, always.

Subtext is another thinking skill that tends to play heavily
in our perceptions. Subtext is something hidden beneath the
words, said without words, undefined and unseen, but like
the metaphorical "gorilla in the room," it is never unfelt.
Through subtext we infer behaviors, attitudes, beliefs, and
understandings. Consider blogger Beth Hill's example of
subtext, "the woman hides her hands behind her back and
rubs her empty ring-finger, becoming teary-eyed as the
bride is toasted." What is not said in the actual words, but
conveyed through subtext, is the idea that the woman is sad
because she herself isn't married and doesn't have the
bride's happiness. We see subtext heavily modeled in
movies and television shows through cleverly written
words and actions portrayed within the characters played
by actors. Even though we are watching fiction, through
these dramas we learn to utilize this same kind of subtext in
our own "real-life" dramas. We can't take anything at face-
value and we end up over-analyzing everything that people
say or do. Often-times, we interject our own personal
biases into our assessments of meaning, and we regularly
end up suffering over our own thoughts.

The use of subtext, language bias, and differing
perspectives can dilute and even mangle true meaning.
Consider for instance the word 'resolute,' an adjective
generally defined as determined or strong-willed.
Synonyms for 'resolute' include: stubborn,
uncompromising, bold and valiant. Antonyms for 'resolute'
include: afraid, cowardly, cooperative and agreeable. Now

take a moment to consider the human value or character that you have learned about this set of words. Both the synonym list and the antonym list contain words that convey judgement of character yet look at the discrepancy between those words. On the one hand, a resolute person who is strong-willed, stubborn and uncompromising has traits that are not usually admired, whereas a resolute person who is bold, determined, or valiant has traits that society admires and considers desirable. This is an example as to why misunderstandings over simple words are so common. A friend once told me how he got caught in this very trap at a business meeting where he asked his boss for a "dedicated manager to the division." He had been sharing one manager with another division, and recent growth in his division led him to the need of an un-shared manager. The use of the word dedicated was meant as wholly committed to only one division and was only meant to describe the job position. The manager, however, took the comment personally, assumed that he was being described as uncommitted or apathetic, and wouldn't talk to my friend for years. Although words are meant as tools for understanding, they can become misinterpreted and misunderstood quite easily.

We have been taught to pay attention to things like word-choice, tone of voice, and body language as a way to judge the subtext of what people "really" mean. This practice of second-guessing each other's words and actions not only leads to misunderstandings, it can also leave us paranoid about our own words and actions. It seems today that common discourse is filled with fear, manipulation, and deceit. We are living in a situation where open, honest communication is becoming rare and even then, can be misinterpreted as attacks or as lies. Often, the Matrix's focus on ego, strong expectations, and judgmental thoughts becomes the lens through which we communicate. This is how our words and messages end up unheard, twisted, or misunderstood.

Coming to a consensus of understanding is becoming difficult because common sense isn't nearly as common as we would like it to be. When we focus through a Matrix lens, an egoic frame of reference, our conversations rarely have much to do with reaching common understanding. Instead, we tell ourselves stories to gain acceptability or influence. Sometimes, these stories come in the form of vilifying others in an effort to inflate our own egos. Matrix-style "communication" often involves traits such as passive-aggressiveness, dishonesty, arrogance, and defensiveness. Due to these types of Matrix intrusions, we have become afraid to truly talk to one another. The old saying, "it can't hurt to ask" becomes blatantly untrue when ego, bullying, and defensive behaviors are involved. The sentiment that one should not talk about religion, politics, or money was likely created as a result of Matrix fears. We dread the put-downs, gossip, cattiness, mocking, rudeness, and over-all bullying that Matrix conversations tend to have. Some people even feel disrespected if others don't agree with them. In the end, mutual understanding is sacrificed and replaced with a confused sense of delusional thinking.

We are taught a long list of expectations based largely on the rules of each paradigm, and the language paradigm seems to have an abundance of them. The main expectation is that, in order to be "right," we must conform to the rules. We learn things in our paradigms as absolutes of human behavior and then we think that these absolutes dictate the rules for everyone. There are volumes of rules out there, many of them we've never used, either because we haven't learned them or because some rules have nothing to do with our own personal paradigms. Rules can be very tricky.

Even though common sense would tell us that there are many different dialects within our own language, we still believe that language is absolute. We would do well to remember that the rules of language are in essence just guidelines, and not, actual rules.

Paradigm shifts happen regularly within language. The example of "good bye" is one of a myriad of ways that language has shifted as words and ideas go in and out of fashion and even take on new meanings. The acceptance of new social trends often leads to the acceptance of new words and the disuse of old. Take for example the push for equality by women in the 1960's. Before this time, job-titles were based on the perception of whether the job was performed by a man or a woman. Children were taught the terms mailman, fireman, and policeman thereby associating the words with the perception that a man "should" be doing those jobs. Some words held clues as to the gender of the person doing the job, such as waiter or waitress and steward or stewardess. Titles such as doctor or nurse were automatically assumed to be gender-specific; doctors were always portrayed as males and nurses as females. This led to a societal impression that boys could become doctors but not nurses and girls could become nurses but not doctors. Although it did not reflect any natural truth, this kind of thinking did affect the choices and attitudes of many people. Within the feminist movement, there was an understanding that certain words were being used to subjugate women and were considered oppressive to women. Since words and attitudes go together, there was a need to change those job titles. This resulted in a paradigm shift in language, wherein we now teach young children about their community using words such as fire fighter, mail carrier, police officer, flight attendant and server. On this same thread, Sweden is in the midst of a major paradigm shift, recently announcing that it was adding

30,000 new words to its language including a gender non-specific pronoun, as part of an effort to show inclusion of all people by way of language. These are examples of both the power and the flexibility of language. It is important to be careful with our words, to choose with clarity and respect in mind. It is also helpful to understand that words are merely tools, for which we, the people, make the rules; they do not have to rule us. As we push for more kindness and respect in our language towards each other, there has been defensiveness from the ingrained mentality of old. There has been a lot of talk about the value of language that is termed, "politically correct." Over the years, language has evolved to show more respect towards others, especially towards their differences. Some people get frustrated at the inconvenience of having to change their ways of thinking and talking. This symbolizes the struggle between two paradigms; are we better off choosing respectful words or should we be allowed to speak in whatever way we want? Is it a matter of "free speech," or a matter of ideals?

Misunderstandings often occur in communication. We can get so caught up in believing our words are absolutes, that we end up assuming we are correct and others are wrong. If we think back on René Magritte's painting, "The Treachery of Images," we are reminded of the lesson that our minds can often be deceived and confused by our symbolism. Words and other symbols help us to interpret the world around us, but too often those interpretations are mistaken as reality and truth. Our differing perceptions can certainly lead to very different views regarding our understandings in life.

A Choir of Voices
Paradigm of Language

"No one means all he says, and yet very few say all they mean, for words are slippery and thought is viscous." Henry Brooks Adams

"It's a strange world of language in which skating on thin ice can get you into hot water." Franklin P. Jones

"Often it's just a short swim from the shipwreck of your life to the island paradise of your dreams, assuming you don't drown in the metaphor." Robert Brault

"Be not the slave of Words." Thomas Carlyle

"Language is a city to the building of which every human being brought a stone." Ralph Waldo Emerson

"Thought is the blossom; language the bud; action the fruit behind it." Ralph Waldo Emerson

"Language is a process of free creation; its laws and principles are fixed, but the manner in which the principles of generation are used is free and infinitely varied. Even the interpretation and use of words involves a process of free creation." Noam Chomsky

"We have too many high-sounding words, and too few actions that correspond with them." Abigail Adams

"The highest form of ignorance is when you reject something you don't know anything about." Wayne Dyer

PART III
THE MATRIX PARADIGM

"But don't be fooled by the radio,

the TV or the magazines.

They show you photographs

of how your life should be;

but they're just someone else's fantasy."

Styx, The Grand Illusion

Unraveling the Matrix Code

"What is the Matrix? It is a prison for your mind."
Morpheus

There was something about the movie *The Matrix* that eerily reminded me of life. At the time that I first watched it, I couldn't make the connection; I was fairly certain that we don't have wires in our heads and we aren't being controlled by Artificial Intelligence. I had a sense, nonetheless, that some strange force was controlling me and everyone around me. The movie portrayed an illusionary, inauthentic life that was encoded by machines, but perceived as reality by those who were plugged in. This inauthentic life now reminds me of our human condition. To varying degrees, we are controlled by our personal and societal paradigms. We are encoded by society's implicit and explicit teachings, with conformity strongly encouraged through the common practice of rewards and punishments. Our encoding is part of a societal operating agreement and is the basis for our foundational knowledge, beliefs, thoughts, perspectives, and stories. We create life stories, based on our personal biases and assumptions and we often mistake these stories as the truth. Perhaps the imprisonment of humanity seen in the movie was actually meant to make us think about the human condition: the imprisonment of our thoughts by means of the illusions and delusions found in our paradigms.

The Matrix paradigm is one of our society's most dominant and most treacherous. Filled with dark, Machiavellian ideals, it is embraced by people who will stop at nothing to win at the Matrix game of life. When we believe that our thoughts reflect reality and that our expectations are actually personal rights, we often set ourselves up for conflict, disappointment, and resentment. Our expectations become our personal definitions for how we believe people should and should not behave. Within this paradigm, we often believe that other people are wrong when their choices don't agree with our own beliefs. When we feel challenged we find ourselves on high alert, ready to judge and become defensive at any attack, real or imagined. The main distress comes from dark Matrix thoughts that we have about our own selves; those that make us fear that we are far from good enough. Because the Matrix ideals are based on perfection, we often second-guess our worthiness, compelling us to try even harder to convince others that we are good enough. The stories we create, our expectations, and our desires are often taught from a perspective of ego. "It's all about me" is a common expression in society. We crave acceptance and personal control. Validation is sought through an emphasis on looks, accumulations, and accomplishments.

Ego is the key concept of the Matrix paradigm. Research indicates that most Americans are self-absorbed and greatly affected by an extreme focus on ego. Narcissism, impatience, and over-sensitivity are seen as norms. People have difficulty with criticism, but often expect praise and instant gratification. It would be a mistake to put the blame on the individuals themselves; we were encoded with such traits by a society that collectively holds a strong value on ego and self-esteem. We are taught from birth to believe that it is our responsibility to learn society's language, rules, and ideals and then to conform to its standards and norms. This is a daunting task since the rules are ephemeral, always shifting and changing. We learn that ideas and definitions change from setting to setting, from person to person, and from paradigm to paradigm. We see people who seem to have expectations for other people's behavior, and yet they don't always have the same expectations for their own behavior. It becomes quite confusing trying to figure out the right answers in life. Not only are we given a sense that knowing the truth and making the right choices is our personal responsibility, we are also taught that our failures or successes will personally define us. We are being set up for failure by measuring ourselves on an impossible bar of perfection. Within the Matrix paradigm, the focus on being special and unique can turn into feelings of loneliness and rejection. When our own judgmental thoughts attack our egos and deem us to be unacceptable, we can end up hating ourselves. We teach our children that criticism is bad, and that compliments are not only mandatory, happiness depends on them. Ironically, our attempt to find happiness through a focus on ego-boosting has resulted in a plague of societal misery instead. Finding happiness and peace through a focus on ego can be quite the daunting challenge.

Overwhelmingly, our encoding teaches us the importance of being a winner and reminds us how dreadful it is to be a loser. In order to gauge our specialness, we learn to compare ourselves with others, hoping that we are above average, a shining star to be admired above the rest. This paradigm teaches that in order to gain acceptance, we must make something of ourselves, look good, be special, gain material possessions, be celebrated, and earn respect through accolades.

We learn to define ourselves and others through labels, titles, bodies, thoughts, and actions. Furthermore, we believe that we are defined by our choices and our experiences both positive and negative. We feel "finally good enough" when we are being celebrated for our choices, but we feel ashamed whenever we do poorly. The Matrix paradigm holds that in order to be considered worthy, we must have a perfectly acceptable persona. There is pressure to be attractive, funny, well-spoken, well-dressed, knowledgeable, and successful at a respectable job. The proper amount of material accumulations, such as an acceptable house and car, are also looked upon as requirements for being good enough.

Within the Matrix mind-set, judging leads to paranoia and paranoia leads back to judging. When people become judgmental, or when we hear gossip, seeds of paranoia are planted in our minds. These seeds blossom into fear that people will be judging us, finding us unworthy, and sharing their criticisms with others in the form of gossip. Seeds of paranoia are planted with every form of rudeness that is portrayed as admirable. The comic who puts down other people, the bully, the gossip, they all model bad behavior that gets emulated. Experiencing these behaviors can plant seeds of fear, leaving us worried that in the future we too will end up being rejected and ridiculed. Every mean, disrespectful, judgmental comment that we say or witness becomes part of our thinking within the garden of paranoia. We end up turning those judgements back on ourselves as we subconsciously recognize that we are just as flawed in our own ways as the people we judge. Our paranoia leads to an unhealthy self-concept and a life driven by fear, worry, and dissatisfaction.

We are taught to believe that life should work out in fairytale fashion, we should get what we think we deserve, and our expectations should all be met. Author and poet, Mark Nepo, writes, "So often we anticipate a reward for the uncovering of truth. For effort, we expect money and recognition. For sacrifice and kindness, we secretly expect acceptance and love. For honesty we expect justice." Within the Matrix paradigm, we are taught to focus on expecting, desiring, and getting what we want in life. Consequently, we feel the need to control things in order to make that happen. When we don't get what we expect, we have been taught to get upset and suffer.

Praise and celebration are extremely important expectations within the Matrix Mind. Many of us have been taught the notion that we should expect people to notice our shining moments with praise, celebrations, and parades. Some go so far as to take on an air of elitism, acting snobbishly and unaccepting of anything below their personal high standards. Society teaches us that being celebrated is the key to self-esteem. Problem is, when celebrations become expectations, we feel let-down when they don't happen. It has become a societal standard to expect rewards. We've learned to believe that we deserve recognitions, acknowledgements, and special treatments, leaving us miserable when we don't get these things. Our unrealized expectations become premeditated disappointments and suffering. Alas, without expectations there would be far fewer disappointments in the first place.

In our youth, we are explicitly taught expectations about life and ourselves. Many parents and teachers think it is part of their responsibility to train children according to our societal standards and norms. Conformity is very important in our society. In an attempt to manipulate behavior through desires and fear, we tell children to be good and they will get a treat, if not they will get punished. We say things like, "shame on you, you are a bad girl or boy," teaching our children to feel shame and to believe that he or she is personally defined by his or her mistakes. We emphasize success to our children, pressuring them to do well in things like sports and school. This is how the encoding of the Matrix Mind is achieved. Since we have been taught to believe that we are labeled by our actions and our mistakes, we end up with feelings of awkwardness and even incompetence as a result. Much of our self-confidence is built around the goals and expectations that society has dictated for us and our self-esteem is often beholden to the opinions of others. We feel great when we are on the winning end of society's ideals but we feel terrible when we are on the losing end. Shame, guilt, remorse, embarrassment, and fear are felt when we think we aren't good enough; anger and sadness are often felt when we believe that other people have let us down. These thoughts are based on nothing more than the delusional norms of society, and yet they create multitudes of real suffering. Through other people's assessments and judgments, we learn to connect our triumphs and mistakes with our own self-confidence and we end up believing that other people's opinions might actually represent the truth about us.

We are also highly impacted by society's use of the impossible bar of perfection used to measure ourselves and others. Use of this scale leaves us feeling like we are not nearly good enough and we secretly fear that we can never measure up. To convince ourselves and others that we are not losers, we have been taught to try to feel superior through bragging about our achievements, titles, trophies, attractiveness, intelligence, and great choices. It bears repeating that in this paradigm, if you aren't a winner, you are a loser. To feel like a winner, we ask ourselves a very problematic question, "Am I better than average?" The answer entails being better than most everyone else. This is slippery slope kind of thinking because statistically, most of us cannot succeed under such a standard. That means that most of us are being set up for failure. Nevertheless, we try to prove ourselves worthy through narcissism and arrogance. This can also include attitudes such as pettiness, put-downs, shaming, disgust, bullying, mocking, or gossiping. Ironically, although these things are done as an effort to feel worthy of acceptance, they are not even considered admirable traits.

Our societal fears have also compelled us to focus on rule-adherence. I can't tell you how many times I used to wish for a manual to teach me the "right way" to do life. As I searched for the "right" answers, I found many different ways of looking at right and wrong. Nonetheless, I honestly thought that the "correct" rules were out there to be found. Many of us crave rules so that we can "know" right from wrong. Unfortunately, too many of us end up believing that our own version of right and wrong, the one based on our personal set of paradigms, is the absolute truth. That is our "in-the-box" thinking. As previously discussed, words are merely symbols created by people as a means of communicating. The rules for language, equally symbolic, are merely in place for consistency and understanding. Teenagers, poets and musicians are known for doing whatever they want with language, bending and changing the rules at will. Nonetheless, within the Matrix paradigm we find people who complain loudly when rules are not followed. Humorously referred to as the "grammar police," a whole group of people have a problem with typos, punctuation errors, and a particularly popular pet-peeve, using the wrong version of there, their, and they're. It is not unusual for people to take offense when seeing things that, in their perception, go against the rules. From the outside looking in, it would appear that a lot of negative energy is expended over some relatively unimportant examples of rule defiance. It is because we think that rules and the adherence to rules is an important societal ideal, that many of us take offense when our rules are not followed. We can get so focused on rules, that we forget that ultimately they are only symbolic, totally made-up concepts and not universal-truths in the least.

Within the Matrix paradigm, having a conversation can be like a mine field, we never know when someone's attitude will blow-up in our faces. With our egos as our focus, we are often sensitive to insults, both real and imagined. We don't want to be patronized, or have our intelligence insulted. We can become very combative when people put down our beliefs or practices. Anything is possible in the world of inference and ego. We can become so obsessed over getting others to agree with us that we miss out on what others have to say. Sometimes, we end up changing the message completely by twisting the meaning of people's words and by assuming that we are being attacked. Open honest communication can be impossible within the Matrix Mind and even become counter-productive when things break down into the realm of ego-wars where there is never really a victor.

We are taught that people will judge us within the first three to five seconds. Although we accept this as truth, in my opinion, it is an unacceptable norm, based on personal subjectivity. We have learned to worry about the impression that we are making on people. In this ego-driven arena, we are taught to assume the focus is on us and to take things very personally. Consequently, our fears drive us to care very much about what other people think, craving acceptance and dreading rejection. We end up finding things about ourselves that don't meet up to our own standards and then using those things to create our own personal suffering. For a long time, I thought very little about the shoes I wore, for example. As a woman with a size 12 foot, my choices were limited to men's shoes so I took what I could get and gave my shoes little thought. That all changed when a friend told me that people will judge us based on our shoes, then I read a magazine article stating that shoes were the first thing that people noticed about you. Although my choices were still the same, I began to worry about what people were thinking and I started to feel embarrassed and ugly. Each time we hear comments criticizing other people about their looks, deficiencies, choices, and mistakes, we learn not only to fear judgmentalism, but we also learn to be judgmental ourselves. This is part of our indoctrination into the vicious cycle of the Matrix paradigm.

Harsh judgment is common in the Matrix Mind. Our attention is especially perked when we think someone has done something wrong. At these times, the norm is to label people by their errors, failures, and faults using derogatory terms such as idiot, stupid, dumbass, or worse. This is the type of thinking that directly feeds the gossip mills. Gossip comes from judgmental condescending attitudes. Gossip makes it appear like we aren't allowed to make mistakes and that if we do make mistakes, those mistakes define who we are as a person. Within gossip, confirmation bias is used to promote negative behaviors such as judgmental thoughts and unkind opinions. This is how stereotypes and prejudice come about. We learn to fear the thought of others gossiping about us, that we too will end up being portrayed as unacceptable or wrong in some way. We worry about being misunderstood or looking awkward and stupid. Many of us believe that if someone judges us harshly, everyone who listens to that person will also judge us harshly based on nothing more than someone else's delusional untruths. Fear of failure and rejection are created in abundance as a result of judgmentalism.

The Bible says, "Judge (not) lest ye be judged and in the same measure you use to judge others you will be judged." This is how judgment works. When we judge others, we end up setting the bar to judge our own selves. Every time we judge, we plant seeds of paranoia in our own minds. Within the Matrix we first learn to measure ourselves and others on an impossible bar of perfection and then to worry about our faults and our inability to measure up. As a result, we end up suffering. In this way we have become our own worst enemies. We end up growing gardens of paranoia in our thoughts, seeded by every Matrix thought of judgmentalism and unworthiness. The reason why we judge is first and foremost because society has taught us to. It has become a societal norm to focus on ourselves and to compare ourselves to others. We have learned to label people's clothes, shoes, hairstyles, bodies, speech, possessions, and choices as good enough or not good enough. Within these judgmental attitudes, we often see rude and malevolent behavior, such as the Matrix appeal of putting other people down. When someone is dressed in a fashion that is different than society's personal sense of style for instance, it is condemned by haters with comments such as, "what were they thinking?" Shaming is one of the many weapons in the armory of the Matrix.

Society seems to love to shame others. We try to dictate how people should behave through acts of passive-aggressiveness. "You are wearing that?" is another question heard in society as an attempt to subtly shame someone's choice of clothes. Comments such as "When are you going to get married?" or "your biological clock is ticking," are examples of passive-aggressive pressure to conform to "expected" standards. Although these tactics are aggressive behaviors, they give the attacker a delusional mask of kindness to hide behind. It doesn't work though because we have been trained to be supremely sensitive to all personal attacks, even these subtle attacks, and therefore it is also a societal norm to take all perceived attacks very personally.

Defensive behaviors are the arsenal of the Matrix paradigm. With ego as the main focus, and fear of being judged on an impossible bar of perfection always lurking, we often find ourselves in defensive mode. This happens when we consider ourselves unworthy or when reality doesn't conform to our expectations. We tend to respond defensively when we don't get what we desire, when we don't get the recognition we think we should, or when we feel that people are not acting "correctly" according to our expectations. There is a tendency to become ego-blind and narrate the story with thoughts such as, "I deserved that" or "How dare they?" Our defenses can be at their worst when we think we are being attacked. We especially hate it when people tell us we are wrong. The fragile ego that secretly fears it is not good enough can become devastated by failure or mistakes. Defensive behavior is the ego's main reaction to those threats. Within the Matrix paradigm, we abhor critiques and corrections. We see them as indicators of our own personal faults. Criticism often brings out defensive behaviors and leads to thoughts such as "Really? That is a stupid way to look at things. What an idiot!" while actually inside our minds, we find ourselves doubting our own worthiness. In the Matrix standard, we believe that our mistakes reflect who we are as people and that they can ultimately end up defining us as not good enough or down-right undesirable. We have learned to believe that people will judge us according to our mistakes because that is the kind of society we live in. Our inability to admit we are wrong often leads to denial and dishonesty. Criticism is one of many human interactions strongly correlated to defensive behaviors.

We also become defensive over differing opinions. We want to hold people accountable to our own personal way of thinking. We are taught to be afraid of diversity, afraid of anything that our current beliefs and ideals don't embrace. If a differing perspective is correct or acceptable it could infer that our own perspective is wrong, therefore

we, ourselves, would be wrong. We have learned to dread
the results of being wrong, so we fight to protect our beliefs
and ultimately to protect our egos.

"People never remember the million times you've helped
them, only the one time you don't." We are hard-wired to
notice differences, a skill that can help us survive.
Unfortunately, this skill has been commandeered by the
Matrix mind-set as a way to find fault in others and to feel
better about ourselves. Since we have an expectation that
people will help us, we see their help as normal and
unremarkable, so we take it for granted and forget to notice.
It is when we don't get what we want and expect that we do
take notice and feel disappointment. In this Matrix
landscape our mistakes are often highlighted and mocked
while our successes are easily overlooked. The futility of
being taken for granted adds to the anguish of being
berated.

Instead of learning a healthy way to deal with our
problems, we are taught to get caught up in our victimhood,
our expectations, our personal beliefs, and our rules.
Having a closed mind doesn't help solve the problems at
hand, but can certainly make them worse and at times,
make them devastating. These days, we see people display
more defensive attitudes than ever. We are afraid of honest
communication and confused by its implications. We end
up with problems that may or may not exist and no viable
skill set from which to solve them. Instead, our confused
thoughts can send us into the defensive realm of fight or
flight as a means to protect our egos at all cost.

Fighting is the main tactic for some. Within the Matrix
Mind we have many weapons to choose from including
bullying, threatening, inflicting physical pain, being catty,
insulting, intimidating, condescending, harassing, mocking,

criticizing, gossiping, slandering, blackmailing, complaining, and cheating to win. We see rudeness, hate, and outrage displayed in any number of aggressive or passive-aggressive ways, such as, "I'm just kidding, or am I?" Arguments tend to be an assault on each other's perspective in order to prove righteousness. Within the Matrix, it is commendable to win no matter the means, fair or unfair.

Lashing out in anger is how the ego is taught to roll in the Matrix. It is a societal norm to stand up with indignity against life's perceived injustices by getting mad and getting even. Once, in a music video, popstar Kelly Clarkson portrayed a woman-scorned. In this video, she vandalized her ex-boyfriend's home and walked out with a smug air of righteousness. Instead of understanding that those acts are crimes, viewers are sent the message that those are admirable traits, worthy of emulation. Another example of society's delusional role modelling is the "deserving" slap across the face in retaliation for unacceptable behavior that has often been rendered by both Hollywood movies as well as parents across the country. This type of role-modeling leads to the erroneous idea that these are actually acceptable and even admirable ways of dealing with people we don't agree with in life. When we believe that these are acceptable choices, we open ourselves up to the possibility of being on the receiving end of someone else's bad behavior. I have personally learned that bringing anger into my problems only makes matters worse. When my abusive ex-husband yelled, I learned to yell back; this only escalated the yelling. When he was rude to me, I was rude in return; this only escalated the rudeness. And once, when he was especially rude, I slapped him across the face, just like my mother and Hollywood had taught me. He responded by hitting me back, really hard. He then asked me how I could think it was legitimate to hit him and not get hit in return. How indeed? That was the last time I ever hit anyone. I learned that it is important to live according to my real truths in life no matter what someone else chooses to do. Experience and research have taught me that anger and self-righteousness are lies that we feel comfortable partaking in when we are living the illusional life of the ego.

Many of us abhor and are intimidated by the concept of fighting so we resist our problems through avoidance. "Run away, run away," was one of my favorite lines from *Monty Python's Holy Grail*. As a peace lover, I didn't have the Matrix fighting skills, so I found myself trying to avoid the fear altogether. I learned to avoid controversial problems in many ways including becoming withdrawn and depressed. The instinct to run away is keen when we don't think we have the wherewithal to fight. We can become complacent or apathetic and have self-defeating limitations on ourselves. Norms of running away include: avoidance, distrust, procrastination, addictions, depression, cutting, and suicide.

Faking it, or being a "poser," has become a Matrix option for surviving the fear and angst. Since so much depends on our acceptable ego, society has come up with a myriad of ways to conform and fit-in with expectations. We often put on masks to help us pretend to be the person we think we are supposed to be, or to hide what we are ashamed for others to see. We are afraid that people will discover that we are actually not good-enough and we worry that our inner ugliness will be discovered. Life has taught most of us to hide our thoughts, especially when they are condescending, judgmental, rude, arrogant, angry, and/or hateful. Although we learned to have these thoughts from society in the first place, we are also taught that they are inappropriate to show in public. We end up wearing masks in an effort to fit-in and conform. These deceptions are also seen in our cheating, stealing, betrayals, rationalizations, and excuses. Inside the Matrix paradigm, it is hard to find an "authentic self."

Many of us have also learned and accepted the practice of hiding our perceived faults and our mistakes. Within the Matrix way of thinking, we define people by their actions. That means that unless we are successful, we are failures. Being wrong has become a most unpleasant concept which our defenses will avoid at all costs. We fear that people will dismiss us when we make mistakes, trip-up, or fail. It is a societal norm to notice, point out, and condemn mistakes, errors, and bad-choices of others. Some of us get caught up in judging and gossiping where we learn how rude and hateful people can be when talking about others, and sometimes we are the ones being unkind. Our zest for pointing out the mistakes of others while going to great lengths to keep ourselves from being in error is the topic of the book and Ted talk, *Being Wrong,* by Kathryn Schulz, "As a culture, we haven't even mastered the basic skill of saying, "I was wrong." Schulz points out. This is defensive behavior that we learn to take on as an attempt to protect our sense of self, leading us to a place where we cannot face our own actions with honesty. We all make mistakes. We need to learn how to support each other's failings, but in the Matrix paradigm, we only learn to condemn them.

Telling ourselves a dramatic story of victimhood when life does not meet our expectations is another aspect of the Matrix paradigm. The victim mentality is filled with such things as perpetual unhappiness, excuses, and self-doubt. We expect happiness to be either a destination or a fulfillment of our desires. Because of ego, we end-up relinquishing control of our happiness to the opinions of others. Unfortunately, many of the things that we think are "real life" come from within the realm of the Matrix. Ego drives us to focus on making people like us, validate us, and accept us. We expect other people to treat us with kindness and respect, but we think that we can dictate the exact manner in which this is done. When people don't do what we expect of them, we often become disappointed and resentful. We tell ourselves a story about how people are supposed to treat us and we take on the role of victim when they don't. Jealousy also stems from society's unrealistic expectations. We believe we deserve more out of life than what we are getting. When we see ourselves lacking in the just-desserts that society seems to promise, we feel sorry for ourselves. These negative feelings can lead us down the miserable road of hatred, larceny, or vandalism. Jealousy is thought of as a green-eyed monster, perhaps for the monstrous havoc that can be wreaked on the lives of those involved.

This Matrix experience is responsible for many miserable lives. We feel anxiety and uncertainty about who we are supposed to be and how we are supposed to get along with others. We wonder if there is any meaningful purpose to life. It is not unusual to end up with a negative self-image along with an unhealthy personal outlook. This is often seen in memes such as "I meditate, I do yoga, and I still want to smack some people," and in "Dear Lord, So far today, I've done all right. I haven't lost my temper, I haven't been greedy, I haven't been grumpy. I haven't been nasty. I haven't been selfish or self-indulgent, and I'm thankful for that. But in a few minutes, I'm going to get out of bed and from then on, I'm probably going to need a lot more help." On the bright side, this may indicate that we are looking for a new way to do life. Meantime, it also highlights the difficulty we can have in this life when we focus in the Matrix, how we learn to focus on our own selves in order to ensure our personal happiness and, in contradictory-fashion, end up feeling miserable and angry.

Hardships and heartaches, in the Matrix paradigm, often end up being recorded as painful memories and end up stored in our bodies as negative energy. Every time we evoke these memories, the painful emotion comes right back, driven by the negative energy that is stored inside. Sadly, the cycle of pain and resentment from unfulfilled expectations and desires is part of the social norm. First, we expect life to be a certain way and then we get upset when life happens differently. We are taught to have a problem when things don't work out the way we think they are supposed to. We learn to hold onto this suffering and have a victim mentality as almost a badge of honor. When others don't treat us the way we think we deserve to be treated, we can end up feeling offended and even violated. Worst case, we create stories bemoaning the idea that we "never deserved to be treated that way" and we lock the painful memories away with all of the negative energy. Through victim mentality, we are compelled to dwell on that pain long after any hope of changing the outcome has been extinguished. This Matrix norm, practiced by many, is part of the delusion; there is no healthy reason for us to continually remember past hurts and allow ourselves to be miserable over them. Furthermore, when we carry our past pain into our present day thoughts and personal perspectives, we create a cynical and jaded outlook on life. We are the only ones at this point keeping those stories alive; without our focus those thoughts cease to exist. This perpetual suffering is nothing more than self-induced pain.

Suffering is normal in the Matrix paradigm, and it is becoming rampant as more hurt people turn around and hurt other people in a futile attempt to salvage and protect their egos. We hurt each other within the Matrix Mind through control, power, oppression, bribery, coercion, blackmail, manipulation, expectations, greed, betrayal, stealing, cheating, threatening, inflicting physical pain, cattiness, intimidation, rudeness, condescension, hate, harassment, bullying, gossiping, mocking, cruelty (scapegoat/ throw under bus), criticizing, intolerance, lying, blaming, playing the victim or the martyr, feeling stigmatized, shaming, revenge, greed, and overall selfishness.

Fear often arises from divisiveness. When we become afraid of people who are different than us, we tend to allow ourselves the freedom to be unkind and disrespectful. We have learned to protect and promote ourselves at all costs, even if we hurt someone else. The ends, we tell ourselves, justify the means. Throughout my life, I have seen examples of fear and hate and I have witnessed the societal mocking of many racial, political, and ethnic groups. Family, friends, and media all joined into the choir of insults often under the guise of comedy. Pollock jokes were especially popular in my youth, replaced by the modern day "dumb blonde" jokes. The jokes are basically the same; the only change is the group that is targeted to attack. Group mentality, a "them-versus-us mentality," has been a fear-based story throughout human history. Many people believe that in order to remain in agreement with ourselves, we must be in disagreement with those who are different.

The garden of paranoia continues to grow with thoughts of judgment, ridicule, and rejection. These days many of us are afraid to act, afraid to do or say most anything for fear of offending most anyone. We learn to "walk on eggshells" and to avoid confrontations in our interactions with others. We fearfully try to predict all of the different ways that our actions can be misperceived. Regardless of how hard we try, we can find ourselves navigating conversations as though a mine field. Inside the Matrix perspective, defensive behaviors can certainly feel like stepping on hidden mines. Our Matrix paranoia has us dreading that people are always waiting for us to slip up so that they can reveal to the world how we are far from good enough. These days, there is a profusion of things that we end up believing we "should not do" for fear of being misunderstood. And yet, all too often, before we know it and without intent, we still end up at the losing end of other people's defensive thoughts, perspectives, and stories. Within this Matrix paradigm, there is no route to true happiness.

The Matrix mind can be a calculated mind. When we help someone, expecting something in return, it is not as much an act of kindness as it is a business transaction. In this mind-set, we think along the lines of "how will this help me?" When we go out of our way to help someone, we expect that effort to pay off, sometimes in very specific ways. If the people we are helping don't acknowledge us or behave as we expect, we can become hateful or play the victim. One way or another, our indignant reaction is meant as an attempt to control someone else's choices. In the comedy favorite, *Everybody Loves Raymond*, the lead character, Ray, gave a loan to his destitute brother, Robert, who used the money to go to Las Vegas with the simple explanation that he may never again be able to afford a trip to Vegas. Ray had assumed that his brother would use the money to help with bills and then suffered plenty when Rob didn't do what he expected. We often want to help, but we have learned to help with strings attached. When we help people using Matrix sensibilities, we often do it with ourselves as the main focus.

Media is a big contributor to the Matrix's success, luring us in like a siren's call to a promised haven from this crazy world, it is actually while in the media's grip that we learn the playbook for the Matrix paradigm. We escape into our TVs, computers, and phones - into a virtual world. We are running away, not from the real world, but from the illusional delusional world we have created in our collective minds. Obsession with movies and movie stars is extensive because we think they represent the ideal which we are all supposed to be yearning for: beauty, talent, successes, and riches. We somehow hope that we can escape into their world and live vicariously through their stories. Our surrender into the perspectives of the media leads to our thoughts being encoded by their ideals and stories. While the ego is focusing on trying to create a perfect persona, media and capitalism are modeling and selling that sense of perfection. Narcissism, victimhood, and all other egoic behaviors in the Matrix paradigm are on display regularly throughout our modern media.

Many advertisers go straight for Matrix vulnerabilities hoping to convince us that our lives will not be good enough unless we spend more money. "It's not a pretty grey" is what the hair industry tells us because they want lifetime customers who will feel ugly unless they dye their hair. Numerous businesses and advertisers attempt to make us feel badly about ourselves in order to convince us to spend lots of money on their products. This is intimidation and coercion, in other words, it is bullying. Capitalism, as a paradigm is basically a solid economic model that has helped grow our country. The problem is that because of greed, a large number of people have chosen to unethically manufacture fear by using the concept of ego as a driving force. In the name of profit, businesses will advertise to our desires or Matrix-defined "short-comings" and offer to sell us the "remedy." We are directly taught many of our beliefs, stereotypes, and prejudices through our media. If prejudicial and disparaging stories about being overweight are part of our upbringing, for instance, those subsequent thoughts and beliefs become a part of our personal encoding and our interpretive lens. Through that lens, we judge others based on their bodies and we are more likely to judge our own bodies quite harshly as well. Capitalistic ventures attempt to drive our thoughts by means of audacious advertising. Our wants and desires are manufactured for us with a goal of trying to make us think that we are not good enough unless we comply to these standards. They want us to believe that we need these things in order to feel happy and acceptable. Capitalism is driven by supply and demand. Advertisers have learned that even if there is no demand, they can artificially create one through exploitation of our fragile egos and our self-doubt.

Our economy seems to be based on a lot of hope and hype. When capitalism is combined with the Matrix, money is valued over people. They want to convince you to buy things you do not need by teaching you Matrix values. One of the most glaring examples is the marketing of anti-depressants. First we are taught to be miserable over delusional concepts and then we are taught to believe that we will feel better by taking a pharmaceutical drug. Dr. Bruce Lipton also gives advertisers credit for molding these beliefs through "savvy marketing," even suggesting that their effectiveness could be partially due to the placebo effect. "The more the miracle of antidepressants was touted in the media and in advertisements, the more effective they became. Beliefs are contagious! We now live in a culture where people believe that antidepressants work, and so they do." Author Leo Buscaglia put responsibility on the media for modeling unrealistic ideas of love, stating that we learn about love from "deodorant ads, cigarette commercials, and cosmetic companies." This leaves many of us with the notion that we can find love through egotistic and materialistic means. One local jeweler exemplified this consumeristic way of thinking with the following advertisement, "The only diamond too big is the one on another woman's hand." Jewelers also want to compel us to conform to social norms of romance through advertisements such as this, "More guys pop the question during the holidays than at any other time of the year, so if your girl is dreaming of a wedding proposal we have just the ring for her." These messages put seeds in girls' heads that often lead to disappointment. If her man is not ready to propose on Christmas, no matter how wonderful and thoughtful he tries to be, if she was dreaming of a wedding proposal and is prone to Matrix thinking, she is likely have a miserable holiday. That is how the Matrix mind works; we are trained to both desire and expect, and are often left with disappointment, sadness, and even anger. Advertisers attack us with these invisible weapons that instill guilt and shame for no reason except to take our money.

Having been led to believe that happiness is something that we can buy, we have learned to be a society of consumers. As such, it is the norm to want increasingly more, obeying the advertisers and conforming to the custom of spending and consuming. Late night talk show host, Conan O'Brien, gave a great example of this when he put together a composite of over two dozen news anchors from across the country, all saying virtually the same thing, "It's okay, you can admit it if you've bought an item or two or ten for yourself this holiday season." There was no coincidence that they were all sharing the exact same story, it was an unveiled attempt at manipulating the people of this country. One of the biggest news stories today is whether the media is telling us the truth or manufacturing stories as propaganda. There is no mistaking the fact that advertisers, and media in general, can drive our thoughts and feelings.

In the movie, *Network*, released in 1976, the main character, news anchor, Howard Beale, decided to air his thoughts about the power of television which he called "the most awesome god-damned propaganda force in the whole godless world." The following is a compilation of his monologue on the power that television has on our current condition.

> "(Television) is not the truth. Television is a God damned amusement park. Television is a circus, a carnival, a traveling troupe of acrobats, storytellers, dancers, singers, jugglers, sideshow freaks, lion tamers and football players. We are in the boredom killing business. You're never going to get any truth from us. We will tell you anything you want to hear. We lie like hell …we'll tell you any shit you want to hear. We deal in illusions man, none of it is true…You are beginning to believe the illusions we are spinning here. You do whatever the tube tells you. You dress like the tube, you eat like the tube, you raise your children like the tube, you even think like the tube. This is mass madness you maniacs… you people are the real thing. We (on television) are the illusion. So, turn off your TVs right now."

This movie first aired over forty years ago. The question is: how long will we continue to live a life of illusions driven by nothing more than works of fiction?

Our society's focus on capitalism and consumerism leads many to place a major emphasis on money and material possessions. The Matrix paradigm teaches us that this is a path to success and happiness. Financial considerations have driven many people to put themselves ahead of others, even to the point of treachery. Some people will lie, cheat, and steal to achieve financial benefits. I once worked at a major telephone service provider, calling former-customers and asking them to come back. Although I was very good at my job, I could never make it to the company's highest tier, the President's Club, which was where the greatest rewards were given. I started listening to a few of my peers who were in the President's Club, and found a startling discovery; one-hundred percent of those I listened to were purposely lying to their customers. I asked one of them how she could do that in good conscience and she simply rubbed her fingers together symbolizing money. I soon learned that this practice was allowed to continue because supervisors and managers all profited from those sales; it wasn't long before I quit for ethical reasons. Pope Francis called capitalism "a subtle dictatorship" elaborating that, "Once capital becomes an idol and guides people's decisions, once greed for money presides over the entire socioeconomic system, it ruins society." Many people worry that unsavory capitalism is having a very detrimental effect on the overall well-being of our society.

It is clear that although some of our choices and behaviors might come from the Matrix paradigm, we embrace and emulate choices from a rich variety of additional paradigms. Values such as love and kindness come from our relationship, religion, or human values (e.g. ethics and morals) paradigms. Unfortunately, the Matrix Mind tends to be at its strongest when we are at our lowest. We can sometimes behave badly because we are experiencing severe distress on our bodies. Alcohol, hormone levels, blood-sugar levels, etc. can bring us to places in our repertoire of behaviors that we normally try to avoid. Recently a man who was apparently drunk was videotaped beating up a cab driver. The next day he said, "I'm not like that." It is possible that he was encoded with those violent behaviors at some point in his life and that they surfaced when alcohol no longer kept them inhibited. Currently, there is a candy bar commercial that reminds us that we are not ourselves when we are hungry, which also highlights the idea that our choices are often influenced by extenuating circumstances. At these vulnerable times, Matrix thoughts can bring out the worst of our encoding. Even though we were taught to have dark irritable thoughts, we are also expected to behave well. This is a dichotomy that teaches us that those thoughts are both acceptable and unacceptable. We are supposed to ultimately have self-control over those thoughts, but that can be difficult when we are not at our strongest. Mood, focus, energy, body chemistry, sugar levels, hormone levels, and sleep levels are all overlooked and underappreciated factors in our human condition. Taking these problems and limitations into consideration can help us better understand both others and our own selves.

Entitlement is the belief that special treatment, extra perks, and success are all things we deserve. Within this belief, we can be oblivious to other people's needs, or worse, think that they are less important than our own. The problem with entitlement is that it's based on the unreasonable Matrix premise that we are more special than others, we have special rights, and people should never show us anything other than the utmost respect. Disrespect is seen as a challenge to our self-worth and we will fight to defend our honor. People with entitlement issues are often unable to take criticism and unwilling to accept the idea that things can be done differently. Ideals found within the Matrix often clash with those in other paradigms. In the relationship paradigm for example, we hear ideals such as being a good listener, focusing on other people's wants and needs, and having empathy. Unfortunately, the Matrix paradigm has taught us to focus on ourselves and our own egos. We end up instead, worrying about whether we are being treated right, cared about, or accepted. Often we overlook the paradigms that teach us to care about others because we are too busy focusing on our own selves to notice.

The Matrix paradigm is an umbrella paradigm for some of society's other problematic paradigms such as racism, sexism, genocide, slavery, and terrorism. Consumerism, entitlement, and egoism also find their roots in the Matrix Paradigm. Consumerism is a cultural paradigm that leads people to find meaning, contentment, and acceptance primarily through the consumption of goods and services. This paradigm comes with some relatively unrealistic expectations, as people seem to believe that a consumer has the right to complete satisfaction regardless of the circumstances. It's not uncommon for people to become quite abusive to anyone in their paths. Recently, for example, when an ice cream company recalled their product from shelves across the country due to a Listeria outbreak, one customer, at the grocery store that my son manages, felt she had the right to hold him accountable for the prospect that her daughter might become ill from already having eaten the ice cream, screaming in his face and threatening to sue him personally. Cases such as these demonstrate how an extreme focus on ourselves can keep us from treating others with kindness and respect. Entitlement is the belief that we have the right or absolute privilege to certain things in life and we think that it is acceptable to withhold that same privilege from others. Egoism is the pursuit of self-interest as the highest good. Racism, sexism, genderism, ageism, classism, and ableism are additional paradigms that leave many in our population at the mercy of hateful ideas, rhetoric, and practices. Genocide, slavery, and terrorism are worst case paradigms in the realm of man's inhumanity to man. Many of these paradigms embrace the ideals of egoism, entitlement, and group mentality. This kind of focus leads many to believe they are better and more entitled than others, leading to selfishness, disrespect, and unkindness, standard practices in many of these paradigms.

"If you can't dazzle 'em with brilliance, baffle 'em with bullshit" is a saying I grew up with. Dishonesty is a norm in today's society. The product of dishonesty is mistrust. When we use the Matrix tendencies such as lies, deceits, and omissions, we lose the ability to trust each other. We often do not see the implications of our actions because we are so narrowly focused on ourselves and our personal stories. The Matrix Mind leads to bitterness and futility and clinging to Matrix ideals and practices results in not only fear and suffering, but also leads to a lack of mutual trust. Letting go of these ideals is the path to peace and a true sense of community.

A Choir of Voices
The Matrix Paradigm
page one

"You will never look like the girl in the magazine. The girl in the magazine doesn't even look like the girl in the magazine." Edith Dohmen

"No society wants you to become wise, it is against the investment of all societies. If people are wise they cannot be exploited. If they are intelligent they cannot be subjugated, they cannot be forced in a mechanical life, to live like robots." Osho

"The profit motive, when it is the sole basis of an economic system, encourages a cutthroat competition and selfish ambition that inspires men to be more concerned about making a living than making a life." Martin Luther King Jr.

We have been programmed by pharmaceutical corporations to become a nation of prescription drug – popping junkies with tragic results." Bruce H. Lipton

"The price of anything is the amount of life you exchange for it." Henry David Thoreau

"We have created new idols. The worship of the ancient golden calf has returned in a new and ruthless guise in the idolatry of money and the dictatorship of an impersonal economy lacking a truly human purpose." Pope Francis

"*I believe the reason the mind has so summarily been dismissed in medicine is the result, not only of the dogmatic thinking, but also of financial considerations.*" Bruce H. Lipton

"*We must rapidly begin the shift from a "thing – oriented" society to a "person-oriented" society. When machines and computers, profit motives and property rights are considered more important than people, the giant triplets of racism, materialism, and militarism are incapable of being conquered.*" Martin Luther King Jr.

"*The richer we have become materially, the poorer we have become morally and spiritually. We have learned to fly the air like birds and swim the sea like fish, but we have not learned the simple art of living together as brothers.*" Martin Luther King Jr.

A Societal Tipping Point

*"If you could kick the person in the pants responsible for
most of your trouble, you wouldn't sit for a month."*
Theodore Roosevelt

2,500 years ago, Greek philosopher, Heraclitus surmised
that "change is the only constant in life." Cultures,
societies, and individuals are all prone to change over time.
There is no specific formula as to how or when societal
changes will happen, but there are indicators. In his book,
The Tipping Point, author, Malcolm Gladwell, describes
some of the conditions that help create change. Those
conditions lead to a concept Gladwell calls "the Tipping
Point," which he describes as "that magic moment when an
idea, trend, or social behavior crosses a threshold, tips, and
spreads like wildfire." When we have had enough of our
delusional norms, when our society becomes disillusioned
and disenchanted enough, we will hit a tipping point and
we will put an end to this Matrix madness through
meaningful change.

It seems as though the American dream has become for
many of us, the American nightmare. Our societal
obsession to live a charmed life has backfired and we seem
to be instead living in a culture driven by disappointment,
fear, and hate. We are certainly seeing a plague of suffering
and an appetite for aggression. When things get really bad,
we have the choice to seek out and advocate for change or
to become numb to the affliction and live a life of abject
acceptance. There is an oft-cited experiment in which a
frog was put in a pan of cool water that was slowly brought
to a boil while another frog was put in a pan of hot water.
The frog placed in hot water jumped out right away while
the first frog never realized the danger creeping up on him,

and eventually boiled to death. We need to wake up from this Matrix fog and recognize how dangerous and destructive it can be. If we remain complacent and numb to these detrimental norms and standards, fear will continue to prosper and destroy.

The effects that the Matrix paradigm has had on an individual's psyche and quality of life are extreme. Today, our society is filled with depression, addiction, bullying, confusion, stress, anxiety, disappointment, rejection, and a lot of fear. Fear keeps us from the lessons of failure. It inhibits growth and divides us. Fear promotes misunderstanding and charges the atmosphere with negative energy. We don't think about the implications our egoic actions have on society because we are too focused on ourselves in the first place. A large portion of our society seems to be lost in this egoic monstrous trance, rarely noticing how their selfish or disrespectful choices negatively impact others.

Society at large, much like the individual, has also been greatly affected by the nature of the Matrix paradigm. In treacherous manner, it has divided and conquered many aspects of our humanity. We have been turned against each other and we seem to be largely insensitive to the needs of others. "If it doesn't affect me, then it's not my problem," is the mentality that feeds the power of inequity. Paradigms, such as male privilege, white privilege, and affluent privilege exist at the expense of women, non-whites, and the poor. Greed and consumerism exist at the expense of the general public. We have many issues tormenting society today. Currently, the racial movement known as "Black Lives Matter" is a protest for the right to basic respect and decency, something that should already be in place. Bizarre issues, such as the "affluenza" defense, are being seen in our courtrooms. This was used by a young man who apparently was brought up too rich to know how rules apply to him. We are living in a society that asks the individual to make good choices without being given the proper knowledge or role-modeling.

Many years ago, while firmly entrenched in my own Matrix-minded worries of not being good enough, I started worrying about those who were considered physically ugly by society's standards. Sometimes I would think about all of the stress that I personally endured trying to look good enough and I would wonder about how hard it would be to live while others deemed you "ugly." I worried that it would be impossible to find happiness for such a person because it seemed that the bullying nature of society would make it unbearable. I imagined that the stress I felt to look good must be crushing to those who society considered ugly. Using the impossible bar of perfection, a whole portion of our society is being left out and ostracized by the large group of people who live by these ridiculous standards. Everyone has a right to a meaningful and contributive life, but under the current model, there is good reason for many of us to believe that we will never be good enough. The harmful and contagious behaviors and comments that are distinctions of the Matrix paradigm have developed into a society plagued with suffering and hatred.

Children are known to blurt out embarrassing comments such as, "You're fat!" and people simply attribute these comments to youth. Children haven't yet learned to keep those comments in their heads. Perhaps it's not a matter of children lacking in social inhibition, but rather a matter of them repeating what they hear from their role-models. Children say rude or disrespectful things because they have first heard them, plain and simple. The art of masking inappropriate and disrespectful thoughts does not stop the cycle. It makes no sense that first we teach children inappropriate behaviors and then we teach them to hide those behaviors.

The fight against horrible behavior has led to a surge of self-esteem promotions. Society has reacted to this painful assault on our egos by declaring that everyone is a winner and everyone is fabulous. We shy away from discussions about failing or making mistakes unless it is to reassure someone that they will be a winner and have lots of successes soon. Yes, these words are nice, but are they honest? They actually send the message that mistakes and losses are not really okay, providing more seeds for the garden of paranoia. Ultimately, these unrealistic platitudes keep us from being able to objectively look at our losses and our mistakes as valuable learning lessons. All too often, we are instead left with the delusional message that we are actually nothing more than losers who should feel defensive and ashamed for not having perfect bodies, minds, or lives. I was brought up with the saying, "If you don't have something nice to say, don't say anything at all." This kind of thinking makes it difficult to communicate about anything critical. In a setting where people are only getting compliments and never getting critiques, the compliments become hollow and constructive criticism becomes impossible. People will say things like, "Oh you look beautiful" whether they think you do or not, at which point, the message can become meaningless.

Those in the Matrix trap often end up leading fake, robotic, narcissistic lives. Within this system, we feel compelled to keep up with the Joneses, throw lavish parties, and buy expensive things that we cannot afford, all in an attempt to impress others. We miss out on the opportunity to get to know each other in meaningful ways. Even worse, we don't get a chance to know our real selves. Without the input of millions of authentic people, we also miss out on the creativity and progress that our society might have otherwise benefited from. It is quite likely that the Matrix paradigm has already had a crippling effect on humanity's overall possibilities.

One of the most common and incapacitating aspects of the Matrix afflictions is our breakdown in communication. Paul Newman and Guns and Roses' fans will recognize the line, "What we've got here is failure to communicate. Some men you just can't reach." We can all relate to these words because they describe the Matrix issues that our society is currently suffering under. When we base our words and messages on inaccurate thinking it can get weird and distorted and eventually wreak havoc on communication and relationships. Through a Matrix focus on ego, we often create stories that do not reflect the actual message. We have a tendency to take things very personally and we believe what we think. We become very defensive when questioned because it threatens our ultimate self-worth. We forget to take the view-points of others into consideration or even bother to listen to them in the first place. We find it futile to try to communicate with someone who is determined to twist our words into things we never meant, and we don't want to engage in battles that seems to have more to do with ego than with creating meaningful messages. Our many exposures to attacks using vicious words and attitudes have left us resorting to practices of avoidance in order to let the Matrix monsters sleep. Defensive behaviors lead to practices such as walking on egg-shells, beating around the bush, or complete silence. When we are solely focused on our own thoughts and our own beliefs, we end up shutting everything else out. We are not comfortable engaging in open, honest communication. We are afraid of being wrong. We are afraid of defensive reactions and therefore, we have break-downs of communication all over the place.

And so it goes, in the terrifying world of the Matrix mind, where communication is broken and confusing.

We have learned to focus on getting special things and on having our heart's desires met, insisting that we can only be happy if we get what we are hoping for. In thinking that we deserve to have specific things in life, we lose the ability to see everything else that is special and wonderful. We lose the ability to enjoy life on its terms and people on their terms. We become disappointed and cannot find joy in life as it is. We end up suffering from our delusions and having the value of our real lives stolen from us.

This Matrix paradigm has degraded some of the beautiful things that are part of our culture and our lives. Traditions such as Christmas, birthdays, engagements and weddings have become high stress and high stakes for the people compelled to do things Matrix style. We worry about whether or not things will be good enough and we are let down when things don't work out the way we think they should. The exchanging of gifts has become especially difficult for people suffering from Matrix paranoia. Gift-giving anxiety is a part of our society where we have a need for approval and a fear of being judged critically. The spirit of the holiday or the celebration can become ruined when our desires don't match our realities. Inside the Matrix Mind, we dictate our desires with great details, we buy the fairy-tale that life should shower us in many, wonderful, specific ways. Happiness in the Matrix paradigm ends up being extremely elusive.

It is important that we stop demonizing the individual for transgressions that are practiced as societal norms. In the Affluenza defense, the boy didn't know any better because he had never been taught any better. This is not a problem of the individual as much as it is a predicament of society.

If we want our children to have better lives, we must focus on and teach better ideals and values, remembering always that our personal choices reflect what we truly value and believe. Once there are enough of us making healthier choices, we will live in a society with healthier standards and norms. That's the way it works. We are, after all, the people.

The signs that society is very close to a Tipping Point from out of the Matrix mindset and into something healthier are starting to flourish in our culture. All kinds of voices are starting to speak out against the viciousness plaguing our society. When a reporter degraded the looks of actress Melissa McCarthy for example, she gracefully educated him by stating, "Just know every time you write stuff, every young girl in this country reads that and they just get a little bit chipped away. I just think we tear down women in this country for all of these superficial reasons and women are so great and so strong." She didn't want the reporter to take it personally, calling this trend "an intense sickness," and saying, "I think that it's a bad habit that we've gotten into, and it's not that people are malicious. I just think it's so easy to take a swipe. Just go the other way; build it up." McCarthy is part of a growing movement intent on standing up for change in our societal norms.

There is a real possibility that many of the people suffering from depression have Matrix beliefs and attitudes to blame. Right now, there is big money in the pharmaceutical approach to emotional suffering, but is it really helping us to live happier lives? It doesn't seem to be creating a healthier society, merely more wealth for the drug companies. A less lucrative but healthier solution would be to go to the source of our feelings of powerlessness and inadequacy, the Matrix Mind, and to address our lifestyle changes accordingly. A paradigm shift away from these practices could produce astonishing results across the mental health landscape.

We were taught *how* to do life more than we were taught *why* to do life. A whole generation of us knew that the answer to the question, "why?" was often, "because I said so." We were taught to conform, and not to question our paradigms at home. In the 1960's, the mantra, "Question authority!" became popular. This was radically different from the existing mindset that taught us to revere and obey authority and to mindlessly submit to the wisdom of the experts. The truth of the matter is: even experts are prone to limitations and faulty information. It is quite normal to hear experts change their views about what is healthy or safe. We are starting to understand that although people are quite educated; our knowledge is also limited on a very large scale. We were taught to depend on societal norms and standards to help us make choices, but it is now apparent that many of our paradigms warrant a critical look.

The suffering created within the Matrix paradigm is indeed a societal problem, and yet it is still an issue that begins and ends with the individual. This paradigm is in existence because of the ways that we are taught to think and behave as egoic people. From the crazy talking-head that is always judging to the garden of paranoia filled with fearful thoughts, our minds can take an awful beating. An egoic focus often leads to an inauthentic life based on illusions, delusions, fear, and pain. We end up depending on people to build us up, and giving them the same power to break us down. The worst part of the Matrix is that it robs us of our opportunity to know who we really are as well as making it next to impossible to live peaceful, happy, and meaningful lives. Even though we have come to these practices through no fault of our own, it is up to the individual to first see through the deception and then to choose differently.

A Choir of Voices
Our Societal Tipping Point

"How very little can be done under the spirit of fear."
Florence Nightingale.

"If you judge people, you have no time to love them."
Mother Teresa

"You can't depend on your judgment when your imagination is out of focus." Mark Twain

"For the one who has conquered the mind, the mind is the best of friends; but for one who has failed to do so, his very mind will be his greatest enemy." Srila Prabhupada

"The corporate revolution will collapse if we refuse to buy what they are selling…Their ideas, their version of history, their wars, their weapon, their notion of inevitability. Remember this: we be many, and they be few. They need us more than we need them. Another world is not only possible, she is on her way. On a quiet day, I can hear her breathing." Arundhati Roy

"Till a man can judge whether they be truths or not, his understanding is but little improved, and thus men of much reading, though greatly learned, but may be little knowing." John Locke

"Science suggests the next step of human evolution will be marked by awareness that we are all interdependent cells within the super-organism called humanity." Bruce Lipton and Steve Bhaerman

PART IV
NEW OUTLOOKS

"The best and most beautiful things in life cannot be seen…They must be felt with the heart."
Helen Keller

"Where there is love there is life."
Mahatma Gandhi

"In the end, only three things matter; how much you love, how gently you lived, and how gracefully you let go of things not meant for you."
Buddha

"I have decided to stick to love. Hate is too great a burden."
Martin Luther King Jr.

"A new commandment I give to you, Love one another."
Jesus

Choices

*"If you can meet with triumph and disaster and treat those
two imposters just the same."*
Rudyard Kipling

In the movie, *The Matrix*, Neo was given the choice
between a red pill and a blue pill, symbolizing his option
between two paradigms; the existing paradigm, which was
a complete illusion, or a new paradigm based in reality.
Right now, we are facing a similar choice; do we continue
to acquiesce to the existing paradigm of the Matrix and all
of its illusional delusional madness or do we blaze a new
trail using paradigms that better represent reality and truth?

Since there is no actual box that we are required to think in,
it is possible to be open to the idea that there are a
profusion of different ways to perceive life. That illusional
box of ours is nothing more than a societal construct of
conformity, which exists merely because we, the people,
continue to participate in it. Our cooperation is absolutely
required in order for it to remain alive and relevant. What
if instead, we decide to partake in practices that better
reflect values of inclusiveness and love? Most of us seek
acceptance and want to be treated with kindness and
respect. So, we begin by being that person. Once we are
ready to let go of the delusional mind-set that is focused on
ego, suffering, and hate, we can then learn how easy it is to
live a much more authentic life. Each of us has our own
special talents, skills, and knowledge to bring to the table.
There is no need for us to have it all. It is a terrible
distortion of reality that we must "become somebody" or
that we need to prove ourselves worthy of being treated like
decent human beings. We were born somebody. We are
worthy of basic kindness and respect because we are all
members of one human family. Each and every one of us

has something important to contribute through our natural aptitudes and fascinations. Having the freedom and incentive to use our personal talents in order to pursue our passions is part of what it means to be authentic. An extensive and diverse amount of knowledge and skills is collectively held, taught, and practiced throughout all of humanity. That same diversity is seen in the individuals who, all together, make up the human family. Instead of teaching conformity through coercion and ego, we can choose to be open to practices of mutual positive regard toward one another and toward ourselves. As John F. Kennedy said in his address to the U.N. General Assembly in 1961, "Conformity is the jailer of freedom and the enemy of growth." The chains of conformity that seem to bind us are merely a societal illusion. Many of the problems that bring about fear, anger, and suffering are simply stories created in our own minds. Therefore, the answer is to purposefully choose a healthier perspective.

If we hold fast to a Matrix mind-set and to our willingness to defend ego at all costs, against anything, real or imagined, our society will become increasingly cold and self-centered. Acts of compassion will become increasingly rare. It's not that people don't care; it is just that they are simply too busy processing life through the terms of their egos to notice anyone else. It's not easy though, our encoding is so deeply ingrained that it can be extremely hard for some people to actively let go of those old mind-sets. Clinging to Matrix ideals, results in fear. Letting go of Matrix ideals, results in peace. It may not be an easy choice to make, but it is a life-changing choice, one that can greatly enhance quality of life.

Escape from this toxic Matrix paradigm is only one
paradigm away. Since it is only one of our many
paradigms, we can look to all of the rest for examples of
behavior and choices that are admirable and respectful.
Take the sport's paradigm for example, which teaches and
promotes fun, teamwork, respect for others, and an honest
work ethic. The paradigm of community holds as its key
ideal that we all have much to contribute. These days, our
sense of community is dwindling, but it can still be seen at
its best in times of crisis. In the Colorado Springs, Colorado
area, during the Black Forest fire that burned 509 homes,
evacuated about 38,000 residents, and cost two people their
lives, fire-fighters came in from all over the country to
work 11 hour per day shifts. Meantime, the people of
Colorado Springs came together with love and compassion.
Although we were a community in crisis, a very wonderful
thing happened; we became a community who deeply
cared. Homes were opened up to evacuees and we had so
many people volunteering that many were even being
turned away. Twice a day, during the shift change,
residents would line the road to the fire-fighters' camp,
holding signs of love and gratitude. Community spirit, as it
turns out, can be a very beautiful thing. This is what we
start to see when we let go of the focus on ourselves and

start looking at life from a more inclusive perspective. *The Three Musketeers* by 19th century French author, Alexander Dumas, teaches us the importance of being there for one another. "One for all and all for one," is a good code to live by.

A major problem is that many of us are never taught the healthy choice of examining our thought processes for logic and fidelity. We are not taught to question our premises or our beliefs in terms of whether they make sense for humanity, whether they represent truth, and whether they have a valid place in our lives. Like the roast beef story, we unquestioningly conform to standards that were passed on by people who don't necessarily understand them either. We end-up passing on a life that is dedicated to some very meaningless and painful pursuits.

Our society has long perpetuated the story of victimhood, teaching us to hold onto painful memories like trophies which were earned through our suffering. We learn to cling to agonizing memories as though our suffering is somehow supposed to go on until the situation is rectified; which will almost never happen. We cannot change the past and we cannot dictate how other people will treat us. This is an important concept in Adyashanti's wonderful book, *Falling into Grace*, about putting an end to suffering. He writes, "When we argue with life, we lose every single time – and suffering wins." The painful story that we hold onto months and years later, is no longer part of reality; the reality ceased to exist when the event was over. Instead, the stories remain only in our memories. When we allow those memories and their negative energies to attack us, they become nothing more than a delusional source of pain. We can be so obsessed with control and getting what we are think we "deserve" that we somehow believe that keeping these illegitimate memories alive is a way to stand up for what is right. That is a delusion as well. Keeping painful memories of unrighteous deeds that others have perpetrated against us will not make those other people suffer; it will only rob us of our own possibilities for happiness in the present moment.

Long before I realized that my problems were rooted in this Matrix Mind, I searched high and low for answers to my unhappiness. I read many books and articles within the "enlightenment" genre, and I often saw that the key was to let go of myself. At the time, this made no sense to me at all. On the one hand, I had played the Matrix game and had worked very hard to accumulate a lot of points in the form of degrees, titles, and accolades. I couldn't fathom letting all of my hard work go to waste. On the other hand, I had no idea how I could actually go about the business of letting go of myself. However, with a turn of the kaleidoscope of perspective, I learned that the "me" that they were suggesting I let go of, is simply the concept of the ego that society had encoded into me. I learned that there was a difference between the two concepts: ego and self. Within the concept of ego, we find the need to be good enough. Within the concept of self, we find that we are already good enough. What we end up letting go of is simply the constructs that we have learned about ego, especially the disrespectful and unkind behaviors toward ourselves and others. Instead of focusing on whether or not we are good enough or whether or not our neighbor is good enough, we can shift our focus to accomplishing goals together. No matter how imperfect we are, it is imperative that we learn to treat each other with kindness and respect if we are to escape the Matrix madness.

The interesting thing about letting go of ego is that, at first, very little changes. You are still in your same body with your same knowledge, memories, and skillsets, but now you use your knowledge and skillsets as tools instead of trophies. You still feel driven to do your best but you don't have any guilty feelings when you make mistakes or when you don't succeed at every venture. As a matter of fact, letting go of ego helps you feel free to be the authentic you, without the tethers of the Matrix shame. Free from egoic worries and distractions, it is possible to feel more daring and brave, ultimately able to become the very best version of your true self. This is what it means to be "authentic." With fear, very little is accomplished, but with bravery, anything is possible. It is in fear that we cling to our egos, and it is with bravery that we find our authentic selves.

Some people, no matter how toxic it is, will hold fast to the egoic mind-set because it represents everything they have ever known. Back in the movie, *The Matrix*, Morpheus explains,

> "The Matrix is a system. That system is our
> enemy. But when you're inside, you look around,
> what do you see? Businessmen, teachers, lawyers,
> carpenters. The very minds of the people we are
> trying to save. But until we do, these people are
> still a part of that system. You have to understand,
> most of these people are not ready to be
> unplugged. And many of them are so inured, so
> hopelessly dependent on the system that they will
> fight to protect it."

The same is true for our own Matrix paradigm. It is a personal choice to let go of this mind-set; not everyone is willing to change. As Bruce Lipton writes, "There is no doubt that human beings have a great capacity for sticking to false beliefs with great passion and tenacity." There are people who will not only hold on to egoic ideals, they will be unhappy to see their loved ones change as well. It may be ideal to offer a way to the light, to a place of peace, love, and happiness, but the truth of the matter is that some people will want to stay in that dark place. Like Morpheus told Neo, at a certain point in our conditioning process, we are so connected to the indoctrination of our system that we don't have the mental wherewithal to unplug. No matter how much this message makes sense, some people will misunderstand it completely. Some people are so attached to fear, anger, and especially their egos that they are not interested in changing their thinking. This message will be best understood by those who are tired of the suffering and who are seeking change in the way people treat each other. This message will make sense to those who are tired of the bullying, the judging, the defensiveness, and the depression.

Most people can relate to the idea of an inner struggle between good and bad. The premise of the light side versus the dark has been repeated in stories throughout time. The "force," a familiar concept to fans of the *Star Wars* movies, was based on the concept of light and dark forces. Scientists say that energy is at the core of everything. We can feel negative energy in a room. We even describe the physical attributes of negative energy with sayings such as, "You can cut the tension with a knife." We also know the feeling of positive energy that is brought about by joy and love. The Yin and Yang symbol portrays balance between these energies. Right now, our society is off-balance because of the build-up of negative energy that accompanies Matrix thinking. We can feel the tension, the suffering, the anxiety; and we are not happy. Many of us end up struggling between making good choices or doing what the Matrix promotes. Parents are famous for saying, "Do as I say, not as I do," (which has never stopped a child from emulating the admitted poor choice.) In our society, we see unkind and disrespectful choices in abundance. We also see people suffering from the avalanche of negativity

that has been encoded into our minds. This negative
energy not only hurts our experiences, it hurts our potential.

There is truth in the saying, 'Whether you think you can or
you think you cannot, you are right." Our energy, and the
energy around us, actually changes when we shift our focus
from worrying about our personal selves to enjoying life. It
is that simple. In his groundbreaking book, *The Biology of
Belief*, Bruce Lipton describes how our genes respond
directly to our perceptions. Lipton writes,

> "The fate and behavior of an organism is directly
> linked to its perception of the environment. In
> simple terms, the character of our life is based
> upon how we perceive it. Our responses to
> environmental stimuli are indeed controlled by
> perceptions, but not all of our learned perceptions
> are accurate. Therefore we would be more
> accurate to refer to these controlling perceptions
> as beliefs. Beliefs control biology!"

Through a shift from negative to positive energy, we can
change our energy. This begins by shifting our beliefs.
Change can be a difficult concept, but as we become
convinced that we want no part of the Matrix paradigm we
start to understand that change is necessary. Matrix
thoughts and behaviors are often toxic and ultimately
dangerous. It is time to put that paradigm into the past and
replace it with healthy choices.

***A Choir of Voices**
Choices
page one

"Faith is taking the first step, even when you don't see the whole staircase." Martin Luther King Jr.

"Happiness is a choice, and so is suffering." Don Miguel Ruiz

"Just as a snake sheds its skin, we must shed our past over and over again." Buddha

"No one saves us but ourselves, no one can, and no one may. We ourselves must walk the path." Buddha

"The nonviolent journey is a process of becoming increasingly free from fear." Mahatma Gandhi

"Security is mostly a superstition. It does not exist in nature... Life is either a daring adventure or nothing at all." Helen Keller

"The greatest healing would be to wake up from what we are not." Mooji

"We are made wise not by the recollection of our past, but by the responsibility for our future." George Bernard Shaw

"When you create a problem, you create pain. All it takes is a simple choice, a simple decision: no matter what happens, I will create no more pain for myself. I will create no more problems. Although it is a simple choice, it is also very radical." Eckhart Tolle

"I am determined to be cheerful and happy in whatever situation I may find myself. For I have learned that the greater part of our misery or unhappiness is determined not by our circumstance but by our disposition." Martha Washington

"Blessed is he who expects nothing, for he shall never be disappointed." Alexander Pope

"Forgiveness in no way requires that you trust the one you forgive…forgiveness is first for you, the forgiver, to release you from something that will eat you alive, that will destroy your joy and your ability to love fully and openly." Wm. Paul Young

A Purposeful Paradigm Shift

*"Our country is in danger, but not to be despaired of . . .
On you depend the fortunes of America. You are to decide
the important questions upon which rests the happiness and
the liberty of millions yet unborn. Act worthy of
yourselves." Dr. Joseph Warren, died at Bunker Hill, 1775*

What does the paradigm of American values look like? Our
Constitution tells us that we are all created equal and that
we have the right to life, liberty, and the pursuit of
happiness. Our national anthem tells us that the United
States of America is the land of the free and the home of
the brave. Our patriotism involves norms of respect such as
standing for the National Anthem with our hats off or
saying the Pledge of Allegiance with our hands over our
hearts. We think of ourselves as generally well protected in
this world through the service, and at times sacrifice, of our
collective armed forces. Patriotism, a sign of our national
pride, is seen in our customs and traditions as well. Yet,
even in those things, there is a lot of debate as to what
values we embrace and how. Some say that capitalism and
riches are of primary importance. Others say that values
such as family, good work ethic, and the Golden Rule, "Do
unto others as you would have them do unto you," are
strong guiding forces. There is a lot of disagreement these
days, but one thing is certain, major portions of our society
are being driven by the Matrix paradigm and we would be
well-served to create our own change. We, the people of
the United States of America, have strength and courage as
our backbone and happiness and liberty as our promise. It
is time for us to be brave in order to find a way to free
ourselves from the bondage created by our egos. It is time
for us to wake up from the trance and seek out a

meaningful life filled with strength, comfort, peace, and joy.

Although ideals of caring and empathy are found within some of our paradigms, our societal norms have largely marginalized these as the ego requires most of our attention. Thinking about the lives of others has taken a back-burner to focusing on ourselves. Societal norms do not routinely teach us to think about others, except from an egoic point of view, nor are we encouraged to self-reflect regarding how our actions affect others. In order for meaningful change to occur, we must let go of thinking from our prescribed point of view and begin to experience life in its purity with no pre-conceived notions of how things "ought" to be. Instead of distressing over being accepted and celebrated, we can simply focus on a life dedicated to being the best version of ourselves each and every day. We can build a new societal mind-set that entails treating ourselves and others with kind loving respect. This is what it takes to bring about a new paradigm from which we can learn to become healthy individuals and can build a happier, more vibrant society.

To create a new paradigm, as we trade in ego for a natural sense of self, we learn the excitement of teamwork and collaboration. Values, such as kindness and respect for others, are enhanced and become more important, while self-centered values become irrelevant and disappear. Our strongest most revered values can become the foundation for a paradigm shift. Our conditioned loops, especially those defensive thoughts and behaviors, take time to reprogram, but the new message is easy to adhere to. If we simply decide that in reality, we are all important members of the human family, we can become comfortable with ourselves and others. Our bodies and minds no longer have to be something to brag about or to be ashamed of. Instead, we learn to take care of our bodies to make our journeys easier. We can simply be the best version of ourselves that we are able and not worry about our image. In any situation, all we can bring to the table is our very best, which is subject to change from moment to moment and year to year. Our happiness is found when we stop concerning ourselves with what life owes us and we start concerning ourselves with how we can contribute to the best possible life, not just for ourselves but for everyone we interact with. Once we let go of ego, we don't need to worry about how our actions will be perceived or celebrated. As author Eckhart Tolle reminds us in *The Power of Now,* "Do not be concerned with the fruit of your action – just give attention to the action itself. The fruit will come of its own accord."

Doing our best is all we can ask of ourselves; sometimes we will have fabulous results and sometimes we will fail. Sometimes we will be on our best game and other times we will make mistakes all over the place. We need to understand that life is meant to be experienced and to be learned from. This cannot be done from a perspective of fear. Instead of focusing on the ways that people hurt our feelings, we can learn to understand that those things are simply not important; they do not define us. We don't need to fear other people's perspectives; there is no good reason to take them personally and no reason to assume that we are actually beholden to any sort of Matrix nonsense. We have to let go of our expectations and assumptions for other people. Respect is nice, but we will not get it from everyone. Kindness is wonderful, but we cannot dictate how people should treat us. We are all subject to error and bad days; taking this into consideration goes a long way in helping us learn to be more patient and supportive of ourselves and one another. Once we let go of all of the expectations that have led us astray, we can learn to take life on its own terms, living and experiencing each moment of each day in the most natural way possible.

It does not come easy! The human endeavor will always be a contrast between suffering and celebrations, between loss and gain. Letting go of the conditioning of the Matrix Mind can be quite difficult at times, especially in our most vulnerable moments when our emotions want to run amok. Our minds are filled with the subconscious programing of egoic tendencies, and as conditioned-loops, they continually find their way to the surface until replaced by new habits. As always, practice makes permanent, and it takes a proactive agreement with yourself to practice re-writing your personal code until it becomes permanent. As it turns out, this can be rather simple to do, because we have a personal warning system that goes off when we go into Matrix mode: stress. Whenever anxiety pokes its worrisome head out, it is usually because of ego and control. Our egos want to somehow control the situation differently. Recognizing these futile thoughts for what they are can remind us that we are only in control of our own choices and that life will happen as it will; we can only do our best.

Many of us are looking for a better way to live life. Trends towards better health and peace of mind are popping up everywhere. Two books that were foundational to this one, Michael A. Singer's *The Untethered Soul* and Eckhart Tolle's *The Power of Now* have recently been on the New York Times #1 Bestseller list. These and other books such as *The Biology of Belief* by Dr. Bruce Lipton and *The Four*

Agreements by Don Miguel Ruiz are adding to the conversation that our thoughts and our beliefs determine our health and our quality of life. We are starting to question our life choices and many of us are finding them to be severely lacking. Our obsession with past problems and pains are being replaced by a more meaningful focus on what is happening in the present. Anxiety from trying to find happiness in future goals and desires is being replaced by appreciation for the many wonderful things that we otherwise forget to notice. Healthier foods are being eaten, exercise is popular, and many people have taken up yoga and meditation in an attempt to find peace and happiness.

I have shared many great books that explain this simple way to a healthier mind-set. One such book, The Four Agreements, by Don Miguel Ruiz shares his family's ancient Toltec wisdom. In this amazingly simple format, we find the answers to letting go of our egos. His advice in four simple points is as follows: "Be impeccable with your word. Don't take anything personally. Don't make assumptions. Always do your best." This is really all it takes. Once we allow ourselves to be comfortable and confident that our best is all we can offer, and as long as we are operating through clear and honest communication, we are free to let go of everything else. At that point, there is no reason to take anything personally and no reason to assume that what we think is always true. When we can let go of these things, and let go of all of the expectations that we have of each other, we can learn to appreciate and enjoy life for what it is.

Peace and happiness will remain elusive and anxiety and disappointment will remain strong, so long as we continue with our unhealthy manner of treating ourselves and others on egoic terms. We are all in this together and none of us know exactly what is going on. Our duty is to take care of our bodies and personal responsibilities, and then to live life to its fullest. Every one of us has something important to offer and frailties to overcome. Mistakes and failures are a valid part of life's lessons and can only be learned if we accept our faults and short-comings as part of the natural course of life. "To err is human; to forgive, divine." 18th century poet, Alexander Pope, wrote these words reminding us that all humans make mistakes and that God's example of forgiveness is the best way to deal with them. Allowing room for error is an important precept for future paradigms.

Sometimes, it is necessary to stand up against rude or hateful behavior and advocating for the principles of love and respect is an appropriate and honorable societal norm. This is exemplified on ABC's ethical-dilemma TV show "What Would You Do?" which asks ordinary people to react to things such as bullying or abuse. One episode staged a controversial public scene and filmed the reactions of ordinary people. In one such scenario, a teenaged boy was verbally berating his "mother" when a woman stepped in and told him that his behavior was disrespectful. The boy told the woman to mind her own business to which she replied, "This is my business because you are in a public place and I am a part of the public. Therefore, what you do affects me and everyone else around me." The idea that we are part of a group seems to evade us when we are deeply focused on ourselves. It is time to start looking outside of ourselves to realize that we have a lot to offer as individuals and the importance of reconnecting to the whole. What we do for each other is as important as what we do for ourselves.

Currently we suffer from the limitations of narrow-minded beliefs, a society filled with people who believe they know the answers, and people who believe what they think. Here is a current-day example of how this thinking plays out. It stems from common arguments over how math is being taught in schools. This example begins with a homework problem that recently set social media into a tizzy. The question asks "Can you make 10 while adding 8 and 5?" Because this kind of question does not relate to the math knowledge of many of today's adults, they are often ready to argue that this type of teaching is ridiculous because 8 and 5 are clearly 13…why confuse the matter? We can attack what we disagree with, or we can investigate further. Many social media conversations revolve around the new concepts being taught in elementary schools, such as core math or math sense. A lot of parents are saying that schools are confusing the children, but that is simply an illusion from their own confusion. Children in the learning phase will be unsure of learning concepts until they are mastered. Adults on the other hand, are more confused because they are stuck thinking inside the box, believing that they know everything there is to know about elementary math. The truth of the matter is, math sense is quite weak in our adult population and schools are working to overcome that by teaching math concepts at a much deeper level than most of today's adults ever learned. Without the benefit of this mathematical background knowledge, adults can find these concepts confusing. This is an example of attacking what we disagree with instead of trying to gain understanding. From a math sense point-of-view, the problem is a place value question created to teach the foundational knowledge of bundling groups of ten. Perhaps they could have reworded the question for better clarity "Can you make a bundle of 10 while adding the numbers 8 and 5?" but that would change the depth of thinking that is being taught. The point is that a plethora of possibilities opens up to us once we understand that thinking outside of the box entails letting go of the box. Our personal knowledge is only a fragment of all there is to know. Once we open our minds to endless possibilities, the sky is the limit.

Through this paradigm shift, we can learn to communicate on more meaningful levels. Instead of listening to respond, we can listen deeply to the stories of others. Instead of talking about things that tear us down, we can talk about things that build us up and bring us happiness. Little by little, once we discard our expectations and harsh judgments, our defensive nature will erode away, and we will have the ability to engage in open honest discussions. This is the skill-set required for meaningful collaboration.

We receive one of life's greatest gifts when we refocus our lives from ego to awareness. Instead of a focus on self and on everything that affects us; we can learn to be open and simply aware of what life is offering right now. There really is far more goodness and far less badness than we have been led to believe. Without the mandates of the Matrix for happiness, we can find the pure joy of experiencing life exactly as it is. Without expectations demanding that life should be a certain way, we are left with the enjoyment of the unexpected. We can celebrate diversity and appreciate people exactly the way that they are. Like a pot-luck meal, we each bring what we can, from food dishes to plates and forks. Some people bring a store bought dish, some cook a homemade favorite, and it becomes a beautiful thing when someone with nothing to share can pick some flowers and put them in a can in the middle of the table and still be appreciated. A Matrix minded person would typically see the opportunity to compare and rank people by better and worse contributions. A community minded person sees all contributions as wonderful aspects of diversity; we give what we can. Sometimes our best is the fancy casserole that everyone is raving about and sometimes we can only pick flowers from a field. Without judgment, we can appreciate it all because we know that everyone has brought from the heart. When we show appreciation and acceptance, we are extending respect and love, giving people the freedom to be themselves. A simple choice is to make the decision not to judge, to look for the good in everything and everyone. At that point, we begin to find not only good, but excellence, in interesting and unexpected places.

Another key aspect to getting the most out of this life comes from a sense of appreciation. The Matrix focus on expectations leaves little room for appreciating the things that we have in life. Letting go of expectations while living fully in the present moment brings about an awareness of life and all that there is to be thankful for. The more we slow down to enjoy and appreciate life on its own merits, the more we find we've been over-looking in life. An unimaginable amount of small joys are imbedded throughout life's offerings, and the sooner we stop dictating and start appreciating what comes our way, the sooner we can partake in a serendipitously joyful and meaningful life. As we have seen, our experience of life is based on our focus, and when we allow ourselves to focus on appreciating the amazing gifts that life has to offer, we find a great many things to appreciate in life.

Back when our human population was smaller, there was a stronger sense of collaboration. Humanity's early survival depended on tribal cooperation. People valued each other as an integral part of the whole. As Aristotle said, "The whole is greater than the sum of its parts." This is the principle of cooperation: when we work together, each bringing his, or her, own unique contribution, we can create something far beyond a compilation of individual products. Remember, it is only together that we can build our immense bridges or discover our new horizons. Many people are under the illusion that competition is always a healthy part of productivity and motivation. We have seen just how unhealthy competition can be from a Matrix perspective. Competition is indeed a valuable and viable aspect to several paradigms such as the sports paradigm, but it is certainly not suitable for all occasions. There are many situations in which other options would be better suited, options such as collaboration. Since we crave acceptance and since we are limited in personal skills, knowledge, and strength, the idea of collaboration is ideally suited to many human endeavors. For those who have had bad experiences with group work in school, there might be strong reservations, but keep an open-mind to the idea that we are no longer limited to our old paradigms and egoic issues. Once we have let go of our unreasonable expectations and treat collaboration on a respectful level, it becomes exciting and dynamic. This is where ideas can flow freely and act as a springboard for new ideas. This is how we can confidently come together with good intentions and come out with phenomenal results.

In 2015, Pope Benedict XVI called for the world's religions to come together in the name of peace and tolerance. He stressed a focus on service and said that people should be treated with dignity. Once we start to look outside of ourselves, we start to become more interested in the people around us. We start to see that we are actually needed by the people in our families and our communities, and we discover that this is a wonderful feeling. Whether we open a door for a stranger or shovel snow for an elderly neighbor, our sense of connection matters. Once we become part of something bigger than ourselves, part of a greater whole, we begin to see that our contributions have an impact. We stop worrying about our mistakes and short-comings. There is great freedom and peace found in knowing that our best is appreciated and that it is always good enough.

The Matrix taught us to think in terms of how life serves us, but there is far more meaning and happiness when we trade that perspective for one of living life to its fullest. We end up with a new focus that stays present and aware of the moment. Gone are the worries of past transgressions and future desires. We still have goals, we just use them as a target rather than a destination for happiness and we act upon them through our present choices. When things go wrong, the thing to do is simply learn whatever life is trying to teach us and then we let go of the pain because we understand that there is only misery in holding on. We learn to accept people as they are and to show them genuine love and respect. We also learn to accept life on its terms, to gracefully accept what we cannot change, and to courageously change what we can. We learn how to tell the difference through the knowledge that we can only change ourselves. Once we let go of trying to control how life should be, we start to become comfortable with a life filled with amazing wonders and phenomenal results. Focus, clarity, better communication, and overall productivity are part of the skill-set that comes with this new paradigm. We learn to live from a place of love. The Bible says in Galatians 5:22, "…the fruit of the Spirit is love, joy, peace, patience, kindness, goodness, faithfulness, gentleness, and self-control. Against such things there is no law." Outside of the Matrix paradigm is where these traits are found. When we don't define our happiness by Matrix terms, we start to see that happiness can be found everywhere, and it is a beautiful thing.

The final and perhaps most important aspect of this paradigm shift is the idea that we must teach our children differently. Children need to understand that there are no bad children, only bad choices or mistakes. We need to help children learn that they are already good enough and that they are not defined by their looks, accomplishments, or mistakes; those are just elements in the experience of life. It is up to us to model and emphasize the crucial aspects of unconditional love with a heart for compassion and respect. We must teach our children to be open-minded and respectful to the ideas of others, there are, after all, a myriad of ways to look at things and who really knows where absolute truth can be found? We find our own joy when we help children find joy and excitement in everyday things. When we teach children that they are not expected to be in control of life, only their choices, it brings about peace and comfort. By teaching our children to live life on different terms than the Matrix paradigm, we give them the best opportunity for a happy life.

Imagine a society whose norms and standards center around the concept of love. Imagine a world where people treat each other with the respect and dignity that comes with unconditional love for the entire human family. Imagine living a genuine experience each and every day with nothing to worry about except doing your best. Imagine coming together with friends, family members, neighbors, and co-workers in an attitude of acceptance and cooperation. Imagine a world filled with the kind of peace

and joy that is found within the true spirit of love.
Together, we have the power to make this happen.

A Choir of Voices
A Purposeful Paradigm Shift
page one

"You never change things by fighting the existing reality. To change something, build a model that makes the existing model obsolete." Buckminster Fuller

"The greatest fear in the world is of the opinions of others, and the moment you are unafraid of the crowd, you are no longer a sheep you become a lion. A great roar arises in your heart, the roar of freedom." Osho

"Whatever our path, whatever the color or grain of our days, whatever riddles we must solve to stay alive, the secret of life somehow always has to do with the awakening and freeing of what has been asleep." Mark Nepo

"If the Golden Rule were followed, the world would be a greater place to live. Courtesy is the core of the golden rule." David Evans

"I was once afraid of people saying, 'Who does she think she is?' Now I have the courage to stand and say, 'This is who I am.'" Oprah Winfrey

"We will not build a peaceful world by following a negative path. It is not enough to say we must not wage war. It is necessary to love peace and sacrifice for it." Martin Luther King Jr.

"There are only two mistakes you can make along the road to truth…Not going all the way…and not starting." Buddha

"It does not matter how slow you go so long as you do not stop." Confucius

"Don't forget that in the midst of all your pain and heartache, you are surrounded by beauty, the wonder of creation, art your music and culture, the sounds of laughter and love, of whispered hopes and celebrations of new life and transformation of reconciliation and forgiveness."
Wm. Paul Young

"We have it in our power to begin the world over again."
Thomas Paine

To you, the reader....

I hope this book has provided
food for thought.

I also hope that it leads to the
discovery of other authors who
have given fantastic advice when it
comes to happiness and authentic
living.

I would like to leave you with a few
lasting impressions from,
A Choir of Voices
The Grand Finale...

A Choir of Voices ~ The Grand Finale

Change

"We are what we repeatedly do. Excellence, then, is not an act but a habit." Aristotle

"Life is a series of natural and spontaneous changes. Don't resist them; that only creates sorrow. Let reality be reality. Let things flow naturally forward in whatever way they like." Lao Tzu

"As soon as we begin to transform the ideas we have of ourselves, we get out of our own way, and a door then opens to who and what we really are. We all have this natural yearning for happiness and freedom. At the core, none of us wants to suffer. When our hearts begin to open, it becomes clear that none of us wants to cause anyone else to suffer either." Adyashanti

"Happiness and freedom begin with a clear understanding of one principle. Some things are within your control and some things are not." Epictetus

"In a growth (to) protection continuum, eliminating the stressors only puts you at the neutral point in the range. To fully thrive, we must not only eliminate the stressors but also actively seek joyful, loving, fulfilling lives that stimulate growth processes." Bruce H. Lipton

"It is important for our health and well-being to shift our mind's energy toward positive, life generating thoughts and eliminate ever present, energy draining and debilitating negative thoughts." Bruce H. Lipton

"I've decided to be happy, because it is good for my health." Voltaire

A Choir of Voices ~ The Grand Finale

Collaboration
page one

"Don't ask yourself what the world needs, ask yourself what makes you come alive. And then go do that. Because what the world needs are people who have come alive."
Harold Whitman

"The reward for kindness is not being seen as kind, but the electricity of giving that keeps us alive." Mark Nepo

"Peace can only come as a natural consequence to universal enlightenment." Nikola Tesla

"Interdependence is and ought to be as much the ideal of man as self-sufficiency. Man is a social being. Without interrelation with society he cannot realize his oneness with the Universe or suppress his egotism." Mahatma Gandhi

"You are not a drop in the ocean. You are the entire ocean in a drop." Rumi

"If you want to walk fast, walk alone; if you want to walk far, walk with others." African Proverb

"Remember, we are all affecting the world every moment, whether we mean to or not. Our actions and states of mind matter because we are so deeply interconnected with one another. Working on our own consciousness is the most important thing we are doing at any moment and being love is the supreme creative." Ram Dass

A Choir of Voices ~ The Grand Finale

Collaboration
page two

"The greatest good you can do for another is not to just share your own riches, but to reveal to him his own." Benjamin Disraeli

"A miraculous healing awaits this planet once we accept our new responsibility to collectively tend the Garden rather than fight over the turf." Bruce H. Lipton

"A Family is a place where minds come in contact with one another. If these minds love one another their home will be as beautiful as a flower garden. But if these minds get out of harmony with each other, it is like a storm that plays havoc with the garden." Buddha

"All humanity is one undivided and indivisible family. I cannot detach myself from the wickedest soul." Mahatma Gandhi

"If we have no peace, it is because we have forgotten that we belong to each other." Mother Teresa

"All people are created equal members of one human family." The official philosophy of Key West, FL

A Choir of Voices ~ The Grand Finale

Love
page one

"Love is a force more formidable than any other. It is invisible – it cannot be seen or measured, yet it is powerful enough to transform you in a moment and offer you more joy than any material possession." Barbara De Angelis

"Hatred does not cease by hatred, but only by love. This is the eternal rule." Buddha

"They do not love that do not show their love." William Shakespeare

"Love is the beauty of the Soul." Saint Augustine

"The greatest happiness of life is the conviction that we are loved; loved for ourselves, or rather, loved in spite of ourselves." Victor Hugo

"Love is the crowning grace of humanity, the holiest right of the soul, the golden link which binds us to duty and truth, the redeeming principle that chiefly reconciles the heart to life and is prophetic of eternal good." Petrarch

"The moment you have in your heart this extraordinary thing called love and feel the depth, the delight, the ecstasy of it, you will discover that for you the world is transformed." Jiddu Krishnamurti

"A loving heart is the beginning of knowledge." Thomas Carlyle

A Choir of Voices ~ The Grand Finale

Love
page two

"Love is our true destiny. We do not find the meaning of life by ourselves alone. We find it with another." Thomas Merton

"We can only learn to love by loving." Iris Murdoch

"In our life there is a single color, as on an artist's palette, which provides the meaning of life and art. It is the color of love." Marc Chagall

"Being loved deeply by someone gives you strength, while loving someone deeply gives you courage." Lao Tzu

"Love is patient and kind; is not jealous, or conceited, or proud; love is not ill-mannered, or selfish, or irritable; love does not keep a record of wrongs; love is not happy with evil, but is happy with the truth. Love never gives up; its faith, hope and patience never fail. Love is eternal....there are faith, hope and love, these three; but the greatest of these is love."
I Corinthians 13

References

Adyashanti. <u>Falling into Grace: Insights on the end of suffering</u>. Boulder: Sounds True, 2011. Used with permission. Reprinted with permission.

Ainley, Nik. <u>Keep it together.</u> Licensed use.

Beck, AT., Rush, A. J., Shaw, B.F., & Emery, G. (1979). *Cognitive therapy of depression.* New York: Guilford Press.

Buscaglia, Leo. <u>Love: What life is all about…</u> New York: Fawcett Books, 1972.

Cuomo, Chris. CNN July 13, 2013.

De' Angelis, Barbara. <u>How to Make Love All the Time: Make love last a lifetime.</u> New York: Dell Publishing, 1991. Reprinted with permission.

Dass, Ram. <u>https://www.ramdass.org/being-love/</u> Reprinted with permission.

Dyer, Wayne. <u>Change Your Thoughts, Change Your Life: Living the Wisdom of the Tao.</u> Carlsbad, Ca: Hay House, 2007. Used with permission.

Elder, Linda. "Critical Thinking and Emotional Intelligence." <u>Inquiry: Critical Thinking Across the Disciplines</u> Winter (1996).

Evans, David. My father's words of wisdom.

References

Fisher, Walter R. "Toward a Logic of Good Reason."
    Quarterly Journal of Speech 64 (December
    1978): 376-384.

Fuller, Buckminster. Library.stanford.edu/collections/r-
    buckminster-fuller-collection. Permission to reprint
    courtesy, The Estate of R. Buckminster Fuller.

Gladwell, Malcolm. The Tipping Point: How little
    things can make a difference. New York:
    Little, Brown and Company, 2002. Reprinted with
    permission.

Hari, Johann. "The Likely cause of addiction has been
    discovered, and it is not what you think."
    Huffington Post Politics, 01/04/2016. Reprinted
    with permission.

Hawkins, David. Truth vs. Falsehood: How to Tell the
    Difference. (Chapter 10, America, p. 174.) Carlsbad,
    Ca: Hay House, 2005. Reprinted with permission.

Hayakawa, S.I. Thought and Action. Orlando: Harcourt,
    1990.

Hill, Beth. Subtext—Revelation of the Hidden". The
    Editor's Bog. May 17, 2011.
    http://theeditorsblog.net/2011/05/17/subtext-
    revelation-of-the-hidden/ Reprinted with
    permission.

Hitler, Adolf. Mein Kampf. 1933.

References

King, Martin Luther. Nobel Lecture: The Quest for
    Peace and Justice. December 11, 1964.
    www.nobelprize.org/nobel_prizes/peace/laureates/19
    64/king-lecture.html
    Reprinted by arrangement with The Heirs to the
    Estate of Martin Luther King Jr., c/o Writers House
    as agent for the proprietor, New York, NY. ©1964
    Dr. Martin Luther King, Jr. © renewed 1990 Coretta
    Scott King.

King, Stephen. The Mist. Frank Darabont and Liz
    Glotzer, producers. 2007. Reprinted with
    Permission from Stephen King.

Krishnamurti, J. Think on These Things. New York:
    HarperCollins Publishers, 1964. Content reproduced
    with permission. Permission to quote from the works
    of J. Krishnamurti or other works for which the
    copyright is held by the Krishnamurti Foundation of
    America or the Krishnamurti Foundation Trust Ltd
    has been given on the understanding that such
    permission does not indicate endorsement of the
    views expressed in this publication.

Kennedy, John F. Address to U.N. General Assembly,
    25 September 1961
    https://catalog.archives.gov/id/46820028.

Kuhn, Thomas. The Structure of Scientific Revolutions.
    Chicago: University of Chicago Press, 1962.

References

Lipton, Bruce H. The Biology of Belief: Unleashing the Power of consciousness, matter & miracles. Carlsbad, CA: Hay House, Inc., 2008. Reprinted with permission.

Magritte, René. The Treachery of Images. Belgium, 1929. Reprinted with kind permission from the Los Angeles Museum of Art. © 2017 C. Herscovici / Artists Rights Society (ARS), New York.

Mooji. https://mooji.org. Reprinted with permission.

Nepo, Mark. The Book of Awakening. ©2000 by Mark Nepo. Used with permission from Mark Nepo and Red Wheel Weiser, LLC Newburyport, MA. www.redwheelweiser.com.

Nietzsche, Friedrich; trans. Walter Kaufmann, The Will to Power, p481 (1883-1888).

O'Brian, Conan. https://www.youtube.com/watch?v=TM8L7bdwVaA &feature=player_embedded.

O'Mahony, Edel. Untangling the Myth – Where Science and Spirituality Meet. http://edelomahony.com/ Reprinted with permission.

Osho. Courage: The Joy of Living Dangerously. NY: St. Martin's Griffin, 1999.

Osho. The Goose is Out. http://www.oshorajneesh.com/download/osho-books/responses_to_questions/The_Goose_is_Out.pdf.

References

Paul, Richard W and Elder, Linda. "Exploring Thoughts, Underlying Feelings, and Feelings" Underlying Thoughts, Sonoma College, Santa Rosa California: Center and Foundation For Critical Thinking, 1995.

Pope, Alexander. An Essay on Criticism. 1771. http://www.newsweek.com/pope-francis-criticizes-unfettered-pursuit-money-bolivia-speech-352259.

Ruiz, Don Miguel. The Four Agreements. San Rafael, CA: Amber-Allen Publishing, 1997.

Sadhguru. http://isha.sadhguru.org. Reprinted with permission.

Schulz, Kathryn. Being Wrong: Adventures in the margin of error. New York: Harper Collins, 2010.

Sieczkowski, Cavan. "Melissa McCarthy Schools Critic on Sexism After He Targeted Her Looks;" Huffington Post 05/20/2015 http://www.huffingtonpost.com/2015/05/20/melissa-mccarthy-sexism.

Singer, Michael A. The Untethered Soul: the journey beyond yourself. Oakland: New Harbinger, 2007.

Gurudev Sri Sri Ravi Shankar. Quoted from a public gathering. Reprinted with permission.

References

The Grand Illusion.
    Words and Music by Dennis DeYoung.
    Copyright © 1977 ALMO MUSIC CORP. and
    STYGIAN SONGSL Copyright Renewed.
    All Rights Controlled and Administered by ALMO
    MUSIC CORP. All Rights Reserved.
    Used by Permission.
    Reprinted by permission of Hal Leonard LLC.

The Matrix. Wachowski, Andy, Larry Wachowski,
    Keanu Reeves, Laurence Fishburne, and Carrie-
    Anne Moss. The Matrix. Burbank, CA: Warner
    Home Video, 1999.
    Reprinted with permission from Warner Bros.

TODAY "The Secret Lives of Teens: Kids open up
    about modern day anxieties" 9/17/14.

Tolle, Eckhart. The Power of Now: A Guide to Spiritual
    Enlightenment. Novato, California: New World
    Library, 1999.

Troeger, Thomas.
    www.scribd.com/doc/300334852/Reader-s-Digest-
    USA-2015-05. Reprinted with permission.

Young, Wm. Paul. The Shack. Newbury Park, CA:
    Windblown Media, 2007. Reprinted with
    permission.

About the author

Mary Ann Schultz received a master's degree in communication from the University of Colorado, Colorado Springs. She has taught elementary school for almost twenty years, and Public Speaking at UCCS for three years. She brings her passion for learning and understanding into this societal exposé.